NATURE'S WONDERLAND

ANIMALS AND PLANTS FROM THE US AND CANADA

DK | Penguin Random House

Author Libby Romero
Subject consultant Eric Peterson
Illustrator Abby Cook

US Senior Editor Shannon Beatty
Senior Editor Roohi Sehgal
Project Editor Robin Moul
Editorial Assistance Agey George, Abi Luscombe
Senior Art Editor Roohi Rais
Project Art Editor Polly Appleton
Art Editor Bhagyashree Nayak
Jacket Designer Polly Appleton
Senior Picture Researcher Sakshi Saluja
Senior Production Editor Nikoleta Parasaki
Producer John Casey
DTP Designers Dheeraj Singh, Syed Md Farhan
Managing Editors Monica Saigal, Penny Smith
Managing Art Editor Ivy Sengupta
Delhi Creative Heads Glenda Fernandes, Malavika Talukder
Deputy Art Director Mabel Chan
Publishing Director Sarah Larter

First American Edition, 2022
Published in the United States by DK Publishing
1745 Broadway, 20th Floor, New York, NY 10019

A catalog record for this book
is available from the Library of Congress.
ISBN 978-0-7440-5951-9

DK books are available at special discounts when
purchased in bulk for sales promotions, premiums,
fund-raising, or educational use. For details, contact:
DK Publishing Special Markets,
1745 Broadway, 20th Floor, New York, NY 10019
SpecialSales@dk.com

Printed and bound in China

For the curious
www.dk.com

CONTENTS

4 Nature of the US and Canada

6 Map of the regions

8 About the regions

10 **The northeastern US**

12 About the northeastern US

14 New England

16 Downeast and Acadia

18 The Adirondacks

20 The Mid-Atlantic

22 Chesapeake Bay

24 **The southern US**

26 About the southern US

28 Appalachian Mountains

30 Mammoth Cave

32 South Carolina Lowcountry

34 The Mississippi River

36 The Gulf Coast

38 The Everglades

40 **The midwestern US**

42 About the midwestern US

44 The Superior Upland

46 The Great Lakes

48 The Central Lowland

50 The Ozarks

52 The Black Hills

54 The Great Plains

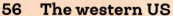
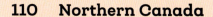

56 The western US
58 About the western US
60 Rocky Mountains
62 The Grand Canyon
64 Mojave Desert
66 Coastal California
68 Pacific Northwest
70 Yellowstone supervolcano
72 Alaska
74 Hawaii

76 Eastern and central Canada
78 About eastern and central Canada
80 The Bay of Fundy
82 The Maritimes
84 Torngat Mountains
86 St. Lawrence Lowlands
88 Niagara Falls
90 Hudson Bay
92 Canadian Shield

94 Western Canada
96 About western Canada
98 The Prairies
100 The Canadian Badlands
102 Banff and Jasper
104 Coast Mountains
106 The Okanagan Valley
108 Pacific Coast

110 Northern Canada
112 About northern Canada
114 The boreal zone
116 Aurora borealis
118 The tundra
120 Ellesmere Island
122 Arctic Archipelago
124 Glossary
125 States, provinces, and territories
126 Index
128 Acknowledgments

NATURE OF THE US AND CANADA

The United States and Canada are paradise for anyone who loves variety in nature. There are polar bears up north and alligators down south. Atlantic puffins fly in the east and giant redwoods grow in the west. Let's explore!

BISON, THE MIDWESTERN US

HOW TO USE THIS BOOK

Exploring the US and Canada has never been easier. Just flip through the pages of this book! You'll learn all about the nature, geography, and wonderful sites found in each country.

DISCOVER SOME OF THE HIGHLIGHTS AND UNIQUE NATURAL FEATURES OF THE REGION.

About the regions

These introductory pages include information about the geography, climate, and habitats in each of the major regions.

North America

The US and Canada cover about 80 percent of the continent of North America. Other places—including Mexico and countries in Central America and the Caribbean—are part of North America, too.

COLD PACIFIC WAVES CRASH ONTO THE ROCKY COAST THAT LINES THE WEST COAST OF NORTH AMERICA.

THERE ARE MANY TALL MOUNTAINS IN NORTH AMERICA. DENALI, IN ALASKA, IS THE TALLEST.

Follow the rules

When you are out in nature, be a smart explorer. Always take an adult with you. Keep your distance from animals, and do not disturb them. Don't touch or eat any plants. Follow the rules on any signs you see. They are there for a reason.

DISCOVER INTERESTING FACTS ABOUT NATURE IN THE STORY BOXES.

THESE LISTS HELP YOU LEARN MORE ABOUT THE AMAZING SITES.

Subregions

Each of the major regions includes famous subregions. These pages catalog some of the wildlife and features found in each one.

Features

If you'd like to learn about amazing natural places in the US and Canada, look no further. These pages tell all about them!

MAP OF THE REGIONS

The United States and Canada are huge countries. To help you explore all the diverse habitats and wildlife they have to offer, we've divided them into seven regions.

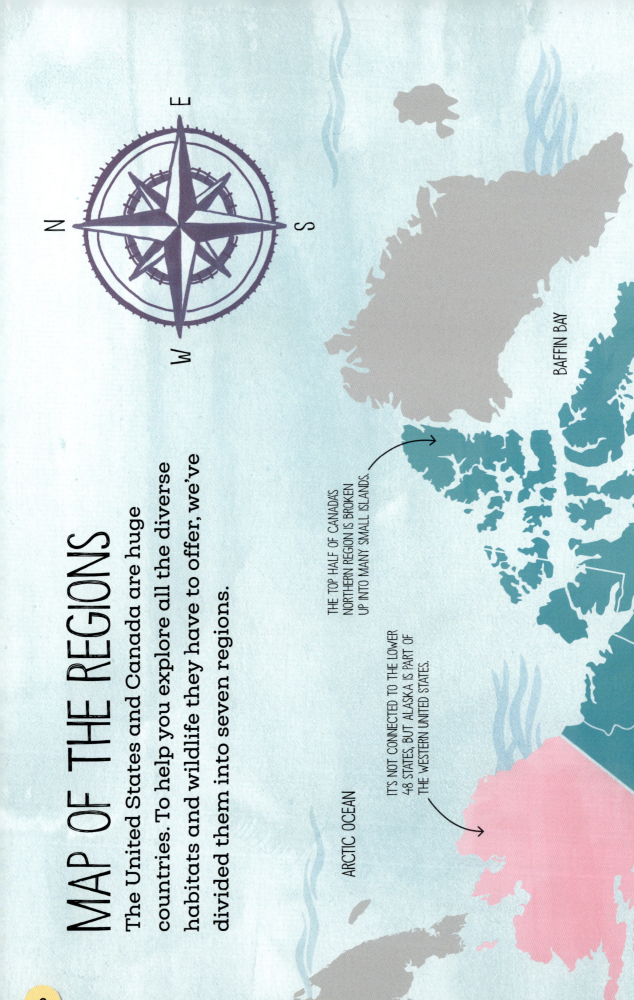

N · E · S · W

THE TOP HALF OF CANADA'S NORTHERN REGION IS BROKEN UP INTO MANY SMALL ISLANDS.

IT'S NOT CONNECTED TO THE LOWER 48 STATES, BUT ALASKA IS PART OF THE WESTERN UNITED STATES.

ARCTIC OCEAN

LABRADOR SEA

BAFFIN BAY

HUDSON BAY

NORTHERN CANADA

6

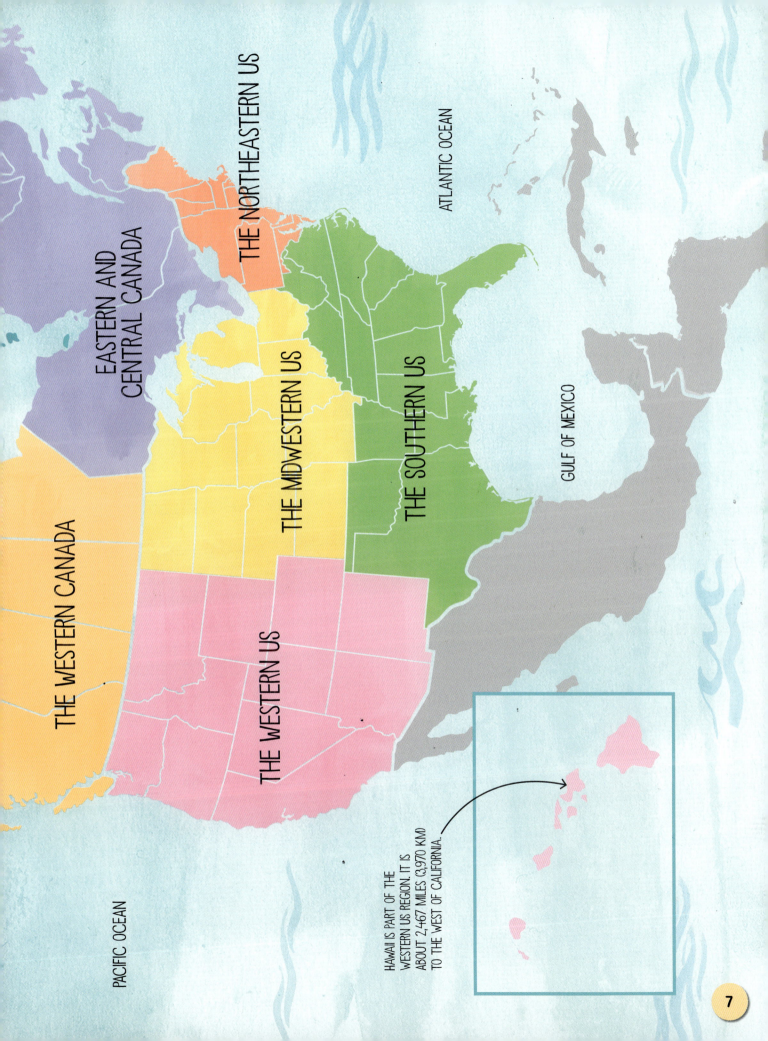

EASTERN AND CENTRAL CANADA

THE NORTHEASTERN US

ATLANTIC OCEAN

THE WESTERN CANADA

THE MIDWESTERN US

THE SOUTHERN US

GULF OF MEXICO

THE WESTERN US

HAWAII IS PART OF THE WESTERN US REGION. IT IS ABOUT 2,467 MILES (3,970 KM) TO THE WEST OF CALIFORNIA.

PACIFIC OCEAN

ABOUT THE REGIONS

The US and Canada make up most of North America. These two countries share many of the same physical features. But regional differences give each country a unique natural identity of its own.

The northeastern US

This region is known for its mountains, rocky coastline, and forests, where red, yellow, and orange leaves blanket the ground every fall.

The southern US

The southern US is a hot and humid place. It is known for alligators, bayous, and sandy beaches that line the coast.

The midwestern US

From the Great Plains to the Great Lakes, the midwestern region has much to offer. Lots of animals, like white-tailed deer, flourish here.

The western US

The western US has many unusual ecosystems. You can see some of the tallest trees in the world in the region's coastal rainforests.

Eastern and central Canada

Eastern and central Canada are covered in important bodies of water, such as Hudson Bay. Lots of water-loving birds and aquatic animals live here.

Western Canada

Canada has lots of beautiful national parks. Banff and Jasper National Parks in western Canada are two of the most impressive.

Northern Canada

Spectacular light shows dance across the night skies in northern Canada. Fewer plants grow here, but many animals roam freely across the landscape.

FALL FOLIAGE, THE ADIRONDACKS

THE NORTHEASTERN US

Stunning fall colors are just one of the delights found in the northeastern US. In this region, you'll also discover rocky ocean shorelines and tall mountain peaks. There are wild horses, blue crabs, and spotted salamanders—not to mention the largest and most biologically diverse estuary in the country.

Major landscapes

Millions of years ago, supercontinents collided and then ripped apart along the eastern edge of the US. Since then, weathering and erosion have carved broad valleys and rolling hills.

IN THE FALL, SPECTACULAR COLORS BURST FROM THE REGION'S MANY FORESTS.

EVERYTHING FROM TINY MICE TO MASSIVE MOOSE LIVE IN THE ADIRONDACK MOUNTAINS.

ABOUT THE NORTHEASTERN US

The northeastern region is the smallest part of the US, but it is packed with natural wonders. There are big, beautiful mountains, rocky Atlantic coasts, and even wild horses!

Water ecosystems

Rivers and lakes provide plenty of freshwater ecosystems in the northeastern US. For saltwater, there's the Atlantic Ocean. In the Chesapeake Bay, you can find both.

WHALES AND OTHER ANIMALS THRIVE IN THE ATLANTIC OCEAN.

CHESAPEAKE BAY IS ONE OF THE MOST BIOLOGICALLY DIVERSE ECOSYSTEMS IN THE WORLD.

NUMEROUS BOGS DOT THE LAND. THEY ARE PRIME LOCATIONS FOR CRANBERRIES TO GROW.

Natural resources

This region has plenty of natural resources, including mountains made of granite, an ocean full of fish, and trees that give us delicious maple syrup!

WILD HORSES ROAM FREELY ON THE BEACHES OF ASSATEAGUE ISLAND.

MOUNT WASHINGTON IS "HOME OF THE WORLD'S WORST WEATHER."

Sites to see

The northeastern US is best known for its fall foliage, rocky coasts, and diverse wildlife. It's also famous for its unpredictable weather.

Mount Washington
Mount Washington is the tallest mountain in the northeastern region. At its summit, people have recorded wind blowing at 231 mph (372 kph) and temperatures dropping to -47°F (-44°C).

NEW ENGLAND

New England is the most northeastern region of the US. Although small, it is quite diverse. Rivers, lakes, mountains, and forests provide plenty of places for plants and animals to live.

Sugar maple
The sugar maple is a tree that grows in cool, moist climates. In the fall, its leaves turn brilliant shades of red, yellow, and orange. People boil its sap to make maple syrup.

EASTERN GRAY SQUIRRELS FLICK THEIR TAILS TO COMMUNICATE WITH EACH OTHER.

Eastern gray squirrel
Eastern gray squirrels typically have brownish-gray bodies with white undersides. But they can also be almost entirely black, particularly in northern regions.

Herring gull
These gulls will do anything to get a meal—even steal food from another bird. Large groups often follow fishing boats in search of scraps.

LOBSTERS CRUSH THINGS WITH THEIR LARGE CLAW AND CUT WITH THE SMALL ONE.

American lobster
American lobsters live in burrows on the ocean floor. They hunt at night when tides are high. If a predator approaches, they quickly flee to their burrows.

EASTERN NEWT SALAMANDER

Big Night migration
Each spring, on rainy nights when temperatures rise above freezing, hundreds of thousands of amphibians emerge from their winter burrows. They travel through the woods to pools of water, where they mate.

North Atlantic right whale
This dark, stocky whale can grow up to 52 ft (15.8 m) long. Blubber (a thick layer of fat that helps to keep an animal warm) accounts for up to 45 percent of its total body weight!

THE NORTH ATLANTIC RIGHT WHALE IS ONE OF THE MOST ENDANGERED WHALE SPECIES.

Spotted salamander
These salamanders live in forests near ponds, where they can lay eggs. They spend most of their time hiding under leaves, logs, or in underground tunnels.

DOWNEAST AND ACADIA

Downeast is part of Maine. It is the easternmost point of the United States. Its rocky shoreline curves in and out of the Atlantic Ocean. Mountains and forests cover the land. Acadia National Park is also a part of this area.

AMERICAN LOBSTER

Lobster fishing

Lobsters are a favorite catch along the Downeast coastline. The waters here are cool and clear. The bottom is rocky. It's the perfect home for these crustaceans.

ACADIA NATIONAL PARK

In the early 1900s, tourists flocked to Acadia. Many people wanted to protect the beautiful landscape. They bought the land and gave it to the federal government. The area is now Acadia National Park.

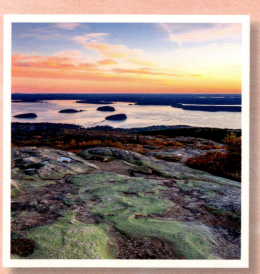

Cadillac Mountain

Cadillac Mountain is the tallest mountain in Acadia National Park. The mountain peak is the first place to see the sunrise in the US.

Along the shores

The Downeast region is made up of peninsulas and islands. Hundreds of harbors and bays are tucked within its shores. Lighthouses stand guard to keep passing ships safe.

LIGHTHOUSES HELP GUIDE BOATS IN THIS AREA OF FOG AND ROCKY CLIFFS.

BURNT COAT HARBOR LIGHT STATION

DID YOU KNOW?

The name "Downeast" comes from the direction some ships sailed to get there: downwind and to the east.

Bubble Rock

Bubble Rock is a massive white granite rock. It sits on the edge of a pink granite mountain. Long ago, glaciers moved Bubble Rock here from 40 miles (64 km) away.

Thunder Hole

When waves rush into Thunder Hole, air and water are forced out. Bang! It sounds like a loud clap of thunder. Whoosh! Water spouts shoot up to 40 ft (12 m) high.

THE ADIRONDACKS

Retreating glaciers sculpted the Adirondack Mountains long ago. Today, the land is filled with forests, wetlands, ponds, and lakes, which provide habitats for a large variety of plants and animals.

Spring peeper
The spring peeper is a tiny tree frog. In early spring, males repeatedly make a high-pitched, single note "peep" sound to call out to mates.

American marten
The American marten is a relative of the weasel. It is a great climber and spends lots of time in trees, although it typically hunts on the ground.

THE CECROPIA SILK MOTH'S WINGS STRETCH NEARLY 6 IN (15 CM) WIDE.

Cecropia silk moth
The cecropia silk moth is the largest moth in North America. It lives in forests and urban areas and can be seen fluttering around porch lights at night.

Kettles
Long ago, huge chunks of glacial ice were buried beneath gravel and sand in the Adirondacks. When the ice melted, it formed round ponds called kettles.

Yellow-rumped warbler

This warbler is a small songbird with a patch of yellow feathers on its rump. It mostly eats insects but munches on berries in the fall and winter.

Cinnamon fern

The cinnamon fern is one of the first ferns to emerge in the spring. It grows in moist, boggy grounds and along streams and shaded ledges.

THE NORTHEASTERN US IN THE FALL

Fall foliage

Each year, people wait for peak season to view the fall foliage in the northeastern US. And with six million acres of protected forests, the Adirondacks is one of the best places to see the beautiful fall colors.

Eastern chipmunk

The eastern chipmunk is a small, striped member of the squirrel family. It can often be seen scurrying around on the ground, gathering food to store for the winter.

EASTERN CHIPMUNKS FEED ON SEEDS AND NUTS.

Pin cherry

This small tree has white flowers that bloom in spring. It's sometimes called a fire cherry because its seeds sprout quickly after a forest fire.

American eel
The American eel looks like a snake, but it's a fish. It is born in the Atlantic Ocean, but lives most of its life in freshwater streams.

Blue crab
As you might suspect, this crab's claws are bright blue. On mature females, the claws also have red tips.

THE MID-ATLANTIC

The Mid-Atlantic region is bordered by the Appalachian Mountains on one side and the Atlantic Ocean on the other. Lush forests, sandy beaches, and the Chesapeake Bay provide homes for all sorts of wildlife.

DID YOU KNOW?
Foxes uses scent to mark their territory. Their scent smells a lot like a skunk!

Red fox
Red foxes are small, doglike mammals. When they hunt, they rely on their excellent senses of sight, hearing, and smell. Once they detect prey, they pounce!

RED FOXES CAN ALSO BE COLORS OTHER THAN RED.

Eastern hemlock

This slow-growing evergreen tree can live for more than 800 years. It typically grows in places with cool, humid climates.

WILD HORSES

American robin

Early in the morning, American robins begin chirping a happy song. Later in the day, you may see one plucking an earthworm from someone's lawn.

Assateague Island

Off the Maryland coast, Assateague Island is well-known for its wild horses. According to local folklore, the first horses here were survivors of a shipwreck. More likely, they were brought here by settlers in the 17th century.

Woodchuck

A woodchuck, also known as a groundhog, is a stocky rodent with a flat head. When threatened by a predator, it quickly dives into its burrow.

THESE FLOWERS CHANGE FROM PINK TO LIGHT BLUE AS THEY MATURE.

Virginia bluebell

These native wildflowers grow in moist woodlands and river flood plains. In mid-spring, loose clusters of blue bell-shaped flowers bloom at the end of arched stems.

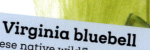

CHESAPEAKE BAY

Chesapeake Bay is the largest estuary in the US, and it's also one of the biggest in the world. It holds about as much water as 27 million Olympic-sized swimming pools. Around 3,600 species of plants and animals live here.

THE CHESAPEAKE BAY BRIDGE

A BLUE CRAB

Blue crabs

Blue crabs are one of the bay's most famous species. They live on the bottom of the bay. Males prefer fresh water. Females like to live near the salty ocean.

CHESAPEAKE BAY FACTS

Length
200 miles (300 km)

Width at narrowest point
2.8 miles (4.5 km)

Width at widest point
30 miles (50 km)

Average depth
21 ft (7 m)

Bay waters

About half the water in the bay comes from the Atlantic Ocean. The other half comes from more than 100,000 rivers and streams in six states.

PROBLEMS AND SOLUTIONS

Millions of people live on land that drains into Chesapeake Bay. They build homes. They fertilize crops, lawns, and gardens. They litter. And when it rains, all of this flows toward the bay.

Polluted waters

When pesticides flow into the bay, they can be harmful to native wildlife. Fertilizers draining into the bay produce algae blooms. These deplete oxygen levels for aquatic life.

Saving the bay

Scientists monitor the bay. Communities host cleanup days. This might not seem like much. But working together, people can have a huge impact on the health of the bay.

MARSH, SOUTH CAROLINA LOWCOUNTRY

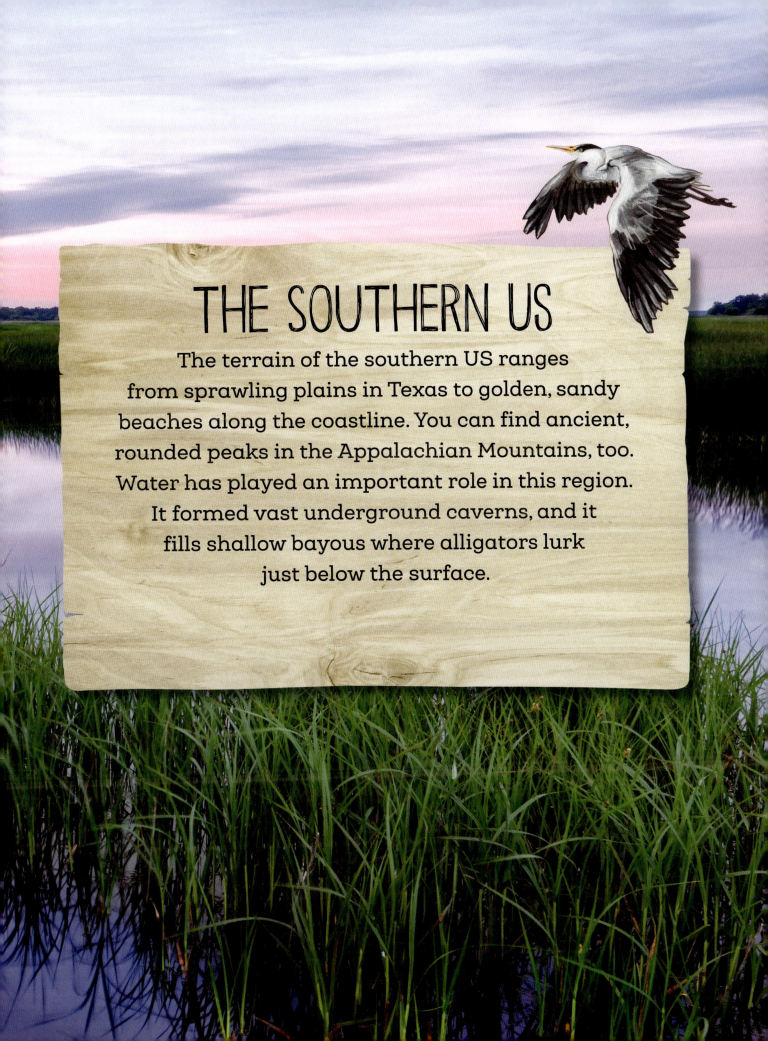

THE SOUTHERN US

The terrain of the southern US ranges from sprawling plains in Texas to golden, sandy beaches along the coastline. You can find ancient, rounded peaks in the Appalachian Mountains, too. Water has played an important role in this region. It formed vast underground caverns, and it fills shallow bayous where alligators lurk just below the surface.

ABOUT THE SOUTHERN US

From the Atlantic shore to the Texas plains, the southern region of the US is full of surprises. At the top of the list are soaring mountains, massive caves, and unique wildlife, such as Florida panthers.

Important ecosystems

In addition to big rivers and the Atlantic Ocean, the southern region of the US has unique water habitats—for instance, bayous and the Everglades.

BAYOUS, SLOW-MOVING CREEKS OR SWAMPS, ARE COMMON IN THE SOUTHERN US.

MANY PLANTS AND ANIMALS LIVE ALONG THE SANDY SHORELINES OF THE ATLANTIC OCEAN AND THE GULF OF MEXICO.

Major landscapes

The southern region is home to two of the most impressive landscape features in all of the US: the Appalachian Mountains and the Mississippi River.

THE MISSISSIPPI RIVER FLOWS DOWN THE MIDDLE OF THE US. IT EMPTIES INTO THE GULF OF MEXICO.

THE APPALACHIAN MOUNTAINS FORMED MILLIONS OF YEARS AGO.

Extreme weather

This part of the US has a subtropical climate. The hot, humid weather and warm ocean waters mean that the area is often hit by hurricanes.

DRIP. DRIP. DRIP. THE SOUND OF NATURE IN ACTION ECHOES OFF THE WALLS AT MAMMOTH CAVE IN KENTUCKY.

HURRICANES ARE EXTREME STORMS THAT CAN STRIKE ANYWHERE ALONG THE ATLANTIC OR GULF COASTS.

Sites to see

The southern region of the US is full of surprises! There are massive caves, ancient mountains, and unique animals that live nowhere else in the US.

THE EVERGLADES ARE HOME TO LARGE PREDATORS LIKE ALLIGATORS AND CROCODILES.

Brown recluse spider

Brown recluse spiders live under rocks, logs, and woodpiles. They can also hide in dark corners of your house. Watch out—they are poisonous!

IT HAS A VIOLIN-SHAPED MARKING ON ITS BACK.

Indigo bunting

Male indigo buntings are blue and flashy. Females are brown. Their dull color helps them hide as they raise their chicks.

APPALACHIAN MOUNTAINS

The Appalachian Mountains stretch for nearly 2,000 miles (3,219 km), from Canada to Alabama. They are home to all kinds of animals and wildflowers.

DID YOU KNOW?

The Appalachians first formed roughly 480 million years ago.

BLACK BEARS ARE GOOD SWIMMERS, GREAT CLIMBERS, AND FAST RUNNERS.

Black bear

Black bears live in large forests, where there are lots of fruits and nuts to eat. When those foods aren't available, they'll eat whatever they can find—even garbage.

Mountain laurel

Mountain laurel is an evergreen shrub that grows up to 15 ft (4.5 m) tall. Its pink-and-white flowers bloom in May and June.

White-spotted slimy salamander

This salamander lives on land, but it has no lungs! Instead, it breathes air through its skin and through membranes in its mouth and throat.

THE SALAMANDER SECRETES A STICKY SUBSTANCE TO DETER PREDATORS.

Salamanders

More salamander species live in the Great Smoky Mountains, part of the southern Appalachians, than anywhere else in the world. The area is often called the Salamander Capital of the World.

YOHAHLOSSEE SALAMANDER

Shagbark hickory

This species of hickory is a member of the walnut family. It is named for its bark, which peels away in large, flat plates.

MAMMOTH CAVE

Mammoth Cave is one natural site that really lives up to its name. With more than 400 miles (643 km) of caverns, this underground maze is the longest cave system in the world.

MAMMOTH CAVE FACTS

Location
Kentucky

Rocks formed
320–360 million years ago

First passages began to form
10–15 million years ago

"Mammoth" passages began to form
1 million years ago

Cave formation

The passages inside Mammoth Cave formed as water dripped through small cracks in the rocks. It took millions of years for the caverns to form.

On the surface

The rolling hills of the Green River Valley lie on top of Mammoth Cave. The Green River helped carve the caverns in the surrounding rock.

THE GREEN RIVER

INSIDE MAMMOTH CAVE

CAVE FEATURES

Time has allowed magnificent features to develop inside Mammoth Cave. Water is always at work, slowly changing the cave.

Stalactites and stalagmites

Dripping water dissolves limestone rocks inside the caverns. This causes icicle-shaped deposits to form. Stalactites hang from the ceiling. Stalagmites form on the floor.

The River Styx

The River Styx is one of the underground rivers that run through Mammoth Cave. When it exits the cave, it flows into the Green River.

THE ANGEL OAK TREE

Spanish moss
This is a rootless plant that wraps itself around trees. Long clumps of its silvery stems dangle from branches all across the Lowcountry.

Angel Oak
The Angel Oak is 65 ft (19.8 m) tall and 25.5 ft (7.8 m) around. Estimated to be more than 400 years old, it is also thought to be one of the oldest living things in the US.

SOUTH CAROLINA LOWCOUNTRY
The Lowcountry is a region along South Carolina's coast. Here, sea islands protect the coast. Warm breezes blow across the marshes and forests, where plants and animals thrive.

THE LOGGERHEAD TURTLE IS THE STATE REPTILE OF SOUTH CAROLINA.

Loggerhead turtle
The largest of all sea turtles, the loggerhead turtle is named after its big head and powerful jaws. Its reddish-brown top shell is slightly heart-shaped.

American oystercatcher
This bird lives along mudflats, beaches, and rocky shores. It pries shells open with its long beak and eats the animals inside.

Sea islands
This string of small islands is scattered along South Carolina's coast. Often separated only by a marsh, the islands protect the mainland from the Atlantic Ocean.

Barking tree frog
Barking tree frogs really live up to their name. When several are together, their calls sound like a pack of barking dogs!

BOBCATS HUNT SMALL RODENTS, RABBITS, AND BIRDS.

TO DETER PREDATORS, ADULTS INFLATE THEIR BODIES WITH AIR SO THEY LOOK BIGGER.

Bobcat
These wild cats have short, or bobbed, tails. Bobcats are stealthy hunters that stalk and pounce on their prey.

Palmetto
A type of palm, the palmetto tree grows on sandy beaches, salt marshes, and coastal woodlands. It is featured on the South Carolina state flag.

THE MISSISSIPPI RIVER

The Mississippi River runs nearly straight south through the middle of the US. It is the second-longest river in North America, after the Missouri, and one of the longest and busiest waterways in the world.

DID YOU KNOW?

It takes about three months for water to travel the entire length of the Mississippi.

MISSISSIPPI RIVER FACTS

Length
2,350 miles (3,782 km)

Width at narrowest point
20–30 ft (6–9 m)

Width at widest point
More than 11 miles (17.7 km)

Volume
About 600,000 cubic ft (17,000 cubic m) of water per second

Major tributaries

The Missouri River and the Ohio River are major tributaries of the Mississippi River. Together, these rivers drain water from 31 US states and two Canadian provinces.

The river's path

The Mississippi begins as a knee-deep creek flowing out of Minnesota's Lake Itasca. At the river's end, it dumps water and soil into the Gulf of Mexico.

FLOWING INTO THE GULF OF MEXICO

THE MISSISSIPPI IN ST. LOUIS, MISSOURI

MIGHTY WATERS

Usually, the Mississippi River flows smoothly as it makes its way south. But when the water rises, watch out! Mississippi River floods can be dangerous.

Mississippi flooding

Heavy rain causes the water level in the Mississippi River to rise. Melting snow does, too. When the river floods, its water can swallow up huge areas of land.

Controlling the Mississippi

People have built walls of dirt, called levees, along the river's edges. When the water level rises, the levees help keep the water in the river.

THE GULF COAST

The Gulf Coast is a large, flat, U-shaped region along the southern coast of the US. It stretches from Florida to Texas. Its landscapes include golden beaches, marshy bayous, and barrier islands.

Great blue heron
A great blue heron moves slowly when it hunts. When it spots a small fish or a mouse, its long neck snaps out fast to snag the prey with its spearlike bill.

Nine-banded armadillo
This armadillo can hold its breath for up to six minutes as it walks across the bottom of a stream. It can also inflate its intestines, which causes it to float!

AN ARMADILLO'S BONY PLATES COVER IT LIKE A SUIT OF ARMOR.

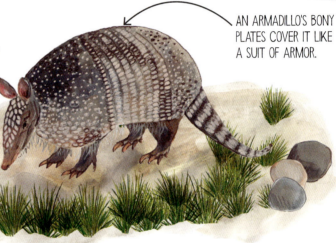

Common bottlenose dolphin
This dolphin can rest one side of its brain at a time. This allows it to swim and come up for air even while it sleeps.

Bayous
Bayous are very slow-moving, marshy waterways. They are often found in shallow rivers, lakes, or estuaries along the Gulf Coast.

Southern magnolia

This evergreen tree has large, glossy leaves that are green on top and rusty brown underneath. Big, fragrant white flowers bloom in the summer.

TINY HAIRS ON THE CRAB'S LEGS TAKE WATER FROM DAMP SAND TO ITS GILLS.

Ghost crab

A white crab uses its large claws to dig burrows on sandy Atlantic beaches. Ghost crabs are scavengers and come out at night to find food.

Ruby-throated hummingbird

This little bird beats its wings more than 50 times per second. It can hover in the air to sip nectar. It can fly upside down and backward, too!

DID YOU KNOW?

A common bottlenose dolphin is very intelligent. Its brain is bigger than a human brain.

A SATELLITE VIEW OF A HURRICANE

Hurricanes

On average, 11 tropical storms form over the warm Atlantic Ocean each year. Six grow strong enough to become hurricanes. Hurricanes often strike the Gulf Coast. Strong winds and storm surges cause massive damage.

THE EVERGLADES

The Everglades is a massive subtropical wilderness in southern Florida. It is filled with cypress swamps, wet prairies, and mangrove forests. It is the perfect habitat for many different water-loving animals to thrive.

American crocodile
American crocodiles live in salt water. They bask in the sun with their mouths wide open to regulate their body temperature. They're shy, but become aggressive if startled.

American alligator
American alligators are mostly found in bodies of fresh water. They use their tails and snouts to dig dens, called gator holes, in the ground.

Marsh rabbit
Marsh rabbits are nocturnal animals, mainly hunted by marsh hawks and great-horned owls. They live near water and are great swimmers. When attacked, they dive into water to escape.

Red mangrove
The red mangrove has roots above and below the water's surface. The prop roots on top filter out salt and supply oxygen to the roots below.

A BURMESE PYTHON

Invasive species

Burmese pythons are exotic animals that were released into the Everglades. They are an invasive species: non-native animals that cause a lot of damage to a habitat. These giant snakes eat all types of animals and have no natural predators.

Florida panther

Florida panthers once prowled throughout the southeastern US. Now, only around 100 panthers remain. Loss of habitat, low numbers, and lack of prey threaten the future of this species.

FLORIDA PANTHERS HAVE LONG LEGS AND SMALL FEET.

West Indian manatee

West Indian manatees live in shallow coastal waters. They graze on seagrasses up to eight hours a day. Sometimes, they dig for roots with their flippers.

WHITE-TAILED DEER, THE GREAT PLAINS

THE MIDWESTERN US

The Great Plains is a key feature of the midwestern US. But this region, which covers the middle of the country, is so much more than grasslands. The Great Lakes line the region's northern borders. The Ozarks rise up in the south. Severe thunderstorms often bring destructive tornadoes, which race their way across the land.

Highs and lows

The midwestern US is dominated by the broad, flat grasslands of the Great Plains. The Ozark Mountains are the only highland, rising about 2,000 ft (610 m) above the plains.

THE OZARKS ARE THE MOST RUGGED HIGHLAND REGION BETWEEN THE APPALACHIAN AND THE ROCKY MOUNTAINS.

AT ONE TIME, BISON ROAMED ALL ACROSS THE GREAT PLAINS. MOSTLY SMALL, PRIVATE HERDS REMAIN TODAY.

ABOUT THE MIDWESTERN US

The midwestern region covers the central part of the US. It's a vast area with many major geographical features. Among them are the Great Plains, Great Lakes, and the mighty Mississippi River.

Bodies of water

Some of the biggest bodies of water in the US can be found in the midwestern region. This includes the Great Lakes and the Missouri and Mississippi rivers.

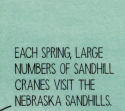

HUNDREDS OF TRIBUTARIES FLOW ACROSS THE GREAT PLAINS INTO THE MISSOURI RIVER.

THE GREAT LAKES HOLD 84 PERCENT OF NORTH AMERICA'S SUPPLY OF FRESH SURFACE WATER.

EACH SPRING, LARGE NUMBERS OF SANDHILL CRANES VISIT THE NEBRASKA SANDHILLS.

Sites to see

Beyond the grasslands, the midwestern US has some stunning sites, including the Black Hills and the Nebraska Sandhills.

THE ANCIENT MOUNTAINTOPS OF THE BLACK HILLS RISE FROM THE PLAINS IN SOUTH DAKOTA AND WYOMING.

PART OF THE MIDWESTERN US HAS SO MANY TORNADOES THAT IT IS CALLED "TORNADO ALLEY."

Extreme weather

This region tends to be hot and humid in the summer and cold and snowy in the winter. It's also known for severe thunderstorms and tornadoes.

Eastern spiny softshell turtle

The Eastern spiny softshell is a large, freshwater turtle. It has a long neck, a snorkel-like snout, and powerful jaws. Its webbed feet are armed with sharp claws.

THE SUPERIOR UPLAND

The Superior Upland lies just south and west of Lake Superior. This area has thick forests, rolling hills, and thousands of lakes that were formed by ancient glaciers.

Monarch butterfly

Monarch butterflies fly south to spend the winter in Mexico. Here, they lay eggs. The next few generations fly back north until they reach the US once more. Then the cycle starts again.

MONARCHS MAKE THE WORLD'S LONGEST INSECT MIGRATION.

DID YOU KNOW?

The Superior Upland region of the US is also part of the Canadian Shield.

Common raccoon

Raccoons can live just about anywhere, as long as they have water and somewhere to hide. Their black masks and ringed tails make them easy to recognize.

Eastern screech owl

These birds are small, gray or red owls with yellow eyes. They eat all sorts of foods—everything from earthworms and crayfish to insects and mice.

SCREECH OWLS MAKE A SCREECHING SOUND.

ONLY MALE MALLARDS HAVE GREEN FEATHERS ON THEIR HEADS.

Mallard

Mallard ducks are found across most of North America. Although they prefer wetlands, they can be found anywhere that has a supply of fresh water—including city parks.

Red pine

The red pine's egg-shaped cones are about 2 in (5 cm) long. Its needles snap and break cleanly when sharply bent. The needles on other pines just fold over.

Northern leopard frog

Typically, northern leopard frogs live close to water. But in the summer, they wander out onto the land. That's earned them a second name—meadow frog.

Gray fox

These foxes live in wooded areas and open brushland. Although primarily nocturnal, they sometimes come out in the day. When chased, they easily climb trees to escape.

A GRAY FOX HAS A BLACK TIP ON ITS TAIL.

Wild sarsaparilla

This small shrub is common in forest understories (just above the forest floor). It produces dark purple berries, and its underground stems can be used to make root beer! (Although, don't try this at home.)

THE GREAT LAKES

Lakes Superior, Michigan, Huron, Erie, and Ontario are the Great Lakes. They hold about one-fifth of all the fresh water on Earth. Their total shoreline is more than 10,000 miles (16,000 km) long.

SURFING ON LAKE SUPERIOR

In the water

The Great Lakes have dangerous currents and regular tides—just like the ocean. They also have waves, which crash onto shore every three to five seconds.

NATURE'S SCULPTURES

The Great Lakes shoreline is a showcase of Earth's history. Arches, caves, and even icicles show how water molds and changes the land around the lakes.

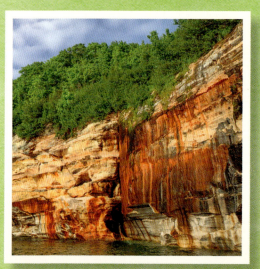

Pictured Rocks
Pictured Rocks are huge cliffs along Lake Superior. As groundwater oozes out of cracks in the cliffs, minerals streak the rock with stains of many colors.

Wildlife

The Great Lakes lie along the Mississippi Flyway, a route birds follow between their breeding and wintering grounds. Billions of migrating birds visit the Great Lakes each year.

A FLOCK OF SEAGULLS AT LAKE MICHIGAN

Icy formations
Freezing temperatures turn lake water into ice sheets, ice balls, and ice volcanoes. Ice caves are another impressive winter creation along the shorelines.

Chapel Rock
Chapel Rock is on the shores of Lake Superior. Water carved this sandstone formation about 3,800 years ago. One 250-year-old white pine tree stands on its top.

Common morel

This mushroom is a prize springtime find in the Central Lowland. It can be used as an ingredient in cooking. It can be spotted growing in moist woodlands and along river banks.

THE CENTRAL LOWLAND

About two million years ago, glaciers inched across parts of the continent. When they melted, they left a giant saucer-shaped region covered by rolling hills and flat plains. This is the Central Lowland.

Muskrat

Muskrats are rodents that live around rivers, lakes, and wetlands. They are great swimmers and can even swim below ice, breathing air trapped under its surface.

THE RED RIVER

Wild turkey

Wild turkeys are plump birds that gobble as they forage for food during the day. They are fast runners and strong fliers. They roost in trees at night.

Lake Agassiz

About 11,500 years ago, Lake Agassiz was the largest glacial lake in North America. But as the glaciers retreated, channels opened, and water drained from the lake. It left behind thousands of lakes and rivers.

White-tailed deer

Female white-tailed deer usually have one fawn at a time. They can have up to four! Newborns have white spots on their fur. The spots disappear by fall.

WHITE-TAILED DEER RUN AWAY AND FLIP UP THEIR TAILS WHEN THEY SENSE DANGER.

DID YOU KNOW?

Male white-tailed deer grow new antlers each spring. The antlers fall off during winter.

Common blue violet

The common blue violet has hairy, heart-shaped leaves and pretty blue, white, or purple flowers. White hairs, called a beard, grow in the middle of the flower, too.

Alligator snapping turtle

Alligator snapping turtles are the largest freshwater turtles in the world. To catch small fish, they wiggle their wormlike tongues. Then, snap! Their powerful jaws slam shut.

Wisconsin Dells

Ancient glaciers carved the Central Lowland—right up to the Wisconsin Dells. After the glaciers melted, the sandstone formations emerged. Weathering and erosion have shaped them ever since.

Big Spring
The Ozarks has many large freshwater springs. Big Spring is one of the biggest in the world. If it ever runs dry, it will leave behind a huge cave.

Largemouth bass
Largemouth bass have great eyesight and hearing. One of their organs can detect vibrations. This helps them feel where prey is moving in the water.

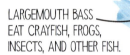

LARGEMOUTH BASS EAT CRAYFISH, FROGS, INSECTS, AND OTHER FISH.

THE OZARKS

The Ozarks is a region of high plateaus in the south-central US. It is filled with forests, rivers, lakes, and caves. A rich variety of plants and animals finds a home in this rugged wilderness.

DID YOU KNOW?
Freshwater jellyfish were accidentally introduced into the Ozarks' lakes.

Coyote
Coyotes are one of the most adaptable animals in North America. They can survive in any habitat—even cities—as long as they can find food.

A COYOTE IS ABOUT THE SAME SIZE AS A GERMAN SHEPHERD.

Water moccasin

Water moccasins are a type of pit viper. They have a heat-sensing pit (a kind of organ) between their eyes and nostrils that helps them zero in on prey. They are venomous snakes.

WATER MOCCASINS ARE ALSO CALLED COTTONMOUTHS. THE INSIDE OF THEIR MOUTHS IS WHITE.

White oak

The white oak is a large, sturdy deciduous tree. Its fruit, the acorn, provides food for many forest animals. In fall, the tree's leaves turn orange and red.

Striped skunk

This skunk has two large scent glands near the base of its tail. When threatened, it bends its behind forward and sprays a foul-smelling fluid as a defense.

AN OZARKS CAVE

Ozark hellbender

The Ozark hellbender is a large aquatic salamander. Adults have lungs, which help them float and sink in the water. They breathe through pores in their skin.

HELLBENDERS CAN SWIM, BUT THEY PREFER TO WALK ACROSS STREAMS AND RIVERS.

Karst topography

The ground beneath the Ozarks is made of soluble rocks. Water easily dissolves them. This type of geology is known as karst topography. It's why the Ozarks area has so many caves, springs, and sinkholes.

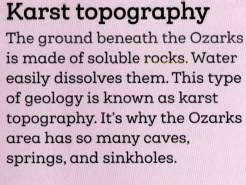

THE BLACK HILLS

Sweeping grasslands cover the Great Plains. But where western South Dakota and northeastern Wyoming meet, ancient mountains rise high into the air. Rounded by time and covered with great forests, these are the Black Hills.

BLACK HILLS NATIONAL FOREST

SACRED LAND

Indigenous peoples—including the Arikara, Crow, Pawnee, Kiowa, Cheyenne, and Lakota—have lived in the Black Hills for more than 10,000 years. Sacred sites in the Black Hills are an important part of their culture.

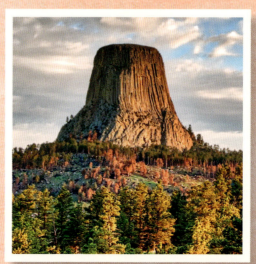

Devils Tower
Known as Mato Tipila in Lakota, this rocky magma column towers above the grassland. For some Indigenous peoples, it is a place to hold ceremonies.

Optical illusion

The Black Hills aren't really black. The mountains are covered with trees that cast shadows on the stones below. This makes the mountains look black from a distance.

PONDEROSA PINE TREES GROW ALL OVER THE BLACK HILLS.

The Badlands

The Badlands lie at the eastern edge of the Black Hills. Long ago, the land here was a warm swamp. Now it looks like the surface of Mars!

COLORFUL HILLS OF THE BADLANDS

Bison
Early settlers hunted the area's bison almost to extinction. This loss was devastating for Indigenous peoples, who depended on bison for their own survival.

Black Elk Peak
Black Elk Peak, the tallest mountain in the Black Hills, is named for Black Elk. This famous Oglala Lakota medicine man had a vision here as a child.

THE GREAT PLAINS

The Great Plains is a vast area that covers the central US. Its grasslands stretch from Texas up to the Canadian border. Animals including lizards and bison have adapted to live here.

Pronghorn

Pronghorns resemble antelopes, but they are their own unique species. Their amazing speed has helped them survive since the days of the saber-toothed cat and woolly mammoth.

PRONGHORNS CAN RUN LONG DISTANCES AT UP TO 60 MPH (96.5 KPH).

Black-tailed prairie dog

Black-tailed prairie dogs dig colonies, called towns. The largest town ever discovered was 250 miles (402 km) long, 100 miles (161 km) wide, and home to 400 million prairie dogs!

Nebraska Sandhills

The Nebraska Sandhills are the largest sand dune formation in the Western Hemisphere. Native grasslands cover most of the dunes, holding them in place.

Texas horned lizard

The Texas horned lizard has some amazing defenses. Its body is covered with horny scales. And if attacked, it can shoot a stream of blood from its eyelids!

THE LIZARD'S COLORING HELPS IT BLEND IN WITH ITS SURROUNDINGS.

Black-eyed Susan

The black-eyed Susan is a common wildflower with bright yellow petals and a dark brown center. It grows quickly and blooms throughout the summer.

Black-footed ferret

The black-footed ferret was thought to be extinct. Then, a colony was discovered. Disease killed most of those ferrets. All black-footed ferrets alive today came from those that survived.

BIG BLUESTEM GRASS

Grass

Grasses are the most notable feature of the Great Plains. Shortgrass, tallgrass, and mixed-grass prairies grow in different parts of the region. They provide food and shelter for animals that live here.

Plains bison

Plains bison are grazers that eat grasses on the Great Plains. Despite their size, they can run up to 35 mph (56 kph) and jump over fences.

REDWOOD FOREST, COASTAL CALIFORNIA

THE WESTERN US

Few regions are more diverse than the western US. It includes deserts in the southwest and coastal rainforests in the Pacific Northwest. Alaska and Hawaii are part of this region, too. With the Rocky Mountains, the Grand Canyon, and Yellowstone's supervolcano, this region showcases some spectacular natural sites.

Highs and lows

Both the highest and lowest points in North America are found in the western US. Denali is a mountain in Alaska, and Badwater Basin is a salt flat in California.

AT 20,310 FT (6,190 M) ABOVE SEA LEVEL, DENALI IS THE THIRD TALLEST MOUNTAIN IN THE WORLD.

BADWATER BASIN IS IN DEATH VALLEY. IT IS 282 FT (86 M) BELOW SEA LEVEL.

ABOUT THE WESTERN US

It would be hard to find a place with more variety than the western United States. Here, you'll find mountains and deserts along with icebergs and rainforests. The climate is just as varied. There are natural hazards, such as earthquakes and volcanoes, too.

MORE THAN 10,000 UNIQUE SPECIES OF PLANTS AND ANIMALS LIVE IN HAWAII'S TROPICAL RAINFORESTS.

Important ecosystems

With so many different types of geography, the western US supports just about every type of ecosystem. Plants and animals have adapted to survive wherever they live.

SPLIT HOOVES HELP BIGHORN SHEEP JUMP AND CLIMB STEEP CLIFFS IN THE ROCKY MOUNTAINS.

Natural hazards

The West Coast of the US is an active place, geologically speaking. It lies along the Ring of Fire, so there are lots of earthquakes. There are plenty of volcanoes, too.

MOUNT ST. HELENS HAD A MAJOR ERUPTION IN 1980.

THE GRAND CANYON IS ONE OF THE SEVEN NATURAL WONDERS OF THE WORLD.

Sites to see

Over time, nature has created two of the most dramatic sites on Earth in this region: the Grand Canyon and Yellowstone National Park.

YELLOWSTONE'S GRAND PRISMATIC SPRING IS THE LARGEST HOT SPRING IN THE US.

Boreal toad
Boreal toads live high up in the mountains. During winter, they hibernate under logs, in beaver dams, or in rodent burrows. Sometimes, many toads stay in one hole.

ROCKY MOUNTAINS

The Rocky Mountains are a major mountain chain in western North America. As the mountains rise, the ecosystems change. The mountains are home to a spectacular variety of wildlife.

A FEMALE BIGHORN'S HORNS ARE HALF AS BIG AS THE MALE'S.

Bighorn sheep
A male bighorn sheep's horns can weigh up to 30 lb (13.6 kg). Rams run toward each other at full speed and crash their horns together to battle for dominance.

Flying saucer clouds

Lenticular clouds often form in the Rockies. These disk-shaped clouds form when stable moist air flows over a mountain. Strong winds hold them in place, making them bob up and down like a UFO (Unidentified Flying Object).

A LENTICULAR CLOUD

Mountain lion
Mountain lions hunt over a large area. They usually ambush prey. Once they catch a meal, they drag it away before eating. They bury leftovers to eat later on.

Peregrine falcon

The peregrine falcon primarily feeds on other birds. It dives very quickly—more than 200 mph (322 kph)—striking prey in midair.

THIS BIRD'S DIVING SPEED MAKES IT THE FASTEST ANIMAL ON THE PLANET!

LOVELAND PASS
ELEVATION 11,990 FT.
CONTINENTAL DIVIDE
U.S. DEPARTMENT OF AGRICULTURE

The Continental Divide

The Continental Divide of the Americas runs from Canada to Mexico. On one side of the divide, water flows to the Pacific Ocean. On the other side, it flows to the Gulf of Mexico.

MOUNTAIN LIONS ARE SOMETIMES CALLED PUMAS, COUGARS, OR PANTHERS.

Ponderosa pine

Ponderosa pines are one of the most fire-resistant trees in the West. When their thick bark catches fire, it falls off. This removes heat from the tree.

THE GRAND CANYON

The Grand Canyon is a deep gorge in northern Arizona. It was formed by the Colorado River and its tributaries. The rivers slowly carved the canyon through layers of rock. Today, the massive canyon is admired for its many shapes and colors.

Wild weather

Huge changes in elevation allow the Grand Canyon to make its own weather. Up high, the North Rim has the coldest, wettest weather. Down low, Phantom Ranch has the warmest and driest.

LIGHTNING STRIKES AN AVERAGE OF 25,000 TIMES A YEAR IN GRAND CANYON NATIONAL PARK.

GRAND CANYON FACTS

Length
270 miles (434.5 km)

Average width
10 miles (16 km)

Widest width:
18 miles (28 km)

Narrowest width
4 miles (6.4 km)

Lowest depth
1 mile (1.6 km)

A STORM AT THE GRAND CANYON

Rocky history

The Grand Canyon is very young compared to the colorful rocks that line its walls. The canyon began to form around 5 to 6 million years ago. Some of the rocks at the bottom are about 1.7 billion years old.

SUNSET AT THE GRAND CANYON

WATER POWER

The Grand Canyon is located in a desert. But water is an important part of its history. Even now, water is at work on the landscape. The water can be beautiful, but it can also be dangerous!

Havasu Falls

Havasu Falls is one of the many waterfalls in the Grand Canyon. It's a beauty! Blue-green water plunges 80 ft (24 m) down a rocky cliff into a pool below.

Flash flooding

Watch out when it rains! Instead of soaking into the ground, the water rushes down into the canyon. It carries mud and truck-sized boulders along with it.

MOJAVE DESERT

The Mojave Desert, located in the southwestern US, is the smallest and driest desert in the country. Temperatures are scorching in the summer, but drop below freezing in winter. Sometimes, it even snows!

Greater roadrunner
Greater roadrunners are weak fliers and fast runners. They spend most of their lives hunting for lizards or small mammals.

Joshua tree
Joshua trees are twisted, spiked yucca plants. They only grow in the Mojave Desert. They rely on yucca moths for pollination.

JOSHUA TREES CAN LIVE FROM HUNDREDS TO EVEN THOUSANDS OF YEARS.

THIS SCORPION GRABS PREY WITH ITS CLAWS AND STINGS IT WITH ITS TAIL.

Giant desert hairy scorpion
The giant desert hairy scorpion is big! It grows up to 7 in (18 cm) long. Tiny hairs on its tail help it feel vibrations to locate prey.

Creosote bush

The creosote bush's roots reach out far in all directions to absorb water. During dry periods, its leaves fold in half—reducing exposure to the sun—to conserve water.

Desert blond tarantula

This large, hairy spider is a reclusive animal. It rarely ventures far from its burrow. Although venomous, its bite is only about as dangerous as a bee sting.

Desert kit fox

Big ears help the desert kit fox hear prey as it hunts at night. They also help the fox stay cool in its underground den during the day.

Death Valley

Death Valley is the lowest, hottest, and driest place in the US. Despite its name, many plants and animals have adapted to survive here.

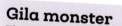

Devils Hole pupfish

This little blue fish only lives in one tiny, hot body of water in the Mojave Desert. It is one of the rarest fishes in the world.

Gila monster

The Gila monster is a venomous lizard. When it bites, its powerful jaws hang tight. As it chews, it releases venom into its prey.

Coast redwood

Coast redwoods are one of the tallest living things in the world. They can grow more than 300 ft (91.4 m) tall. Some trees alive now are thousands of years old.

DID YOU KNOW?

From December to May, around 20,000 gray whales migrate along the California coast.

Gray whale

Gray whales stay in shallow waters close to shore. Their mottled gray bodies are usually covered with whale lice.

COASTAL CALIFORNIA

The California coastal region provides a rich variety of climates and ecosystems. Rocky cliffs, chilly waters, sandy beaches, and forests of towering trees can all be found in this part of the US.

SEA OTTERS HAVE THE THICKEST FUR OF ANY ANIMAL.

Sea otter

Sea otters spend all their time in the ocean. When they sleep, they often wrap themselves in giant kelp. This keeps them from floating away!

Green sea anemone

The green sea anemone looks like a plant, but it's an animal. It can grow to around 11.8 in (30 cm). After it digests its food, a green sea anemone poops out of its mouth!

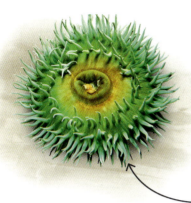

THE ANEMONE STUNS PREY WITH THE TENTACLES AROUND ITS MOUTH.

California sea lion

California sea lions are eared seals. When they rest, they lie motionless and hold their flippers above the water. This behavior is called rafting.

California condor

California condors can fly for hours without beating their wings. After rising thousands of feet in the air, they soar and glide on air currents.

Giant kelp

Giant kelp is the largest species of marine algae. It grows up to 100 ft (30 m) tall and creates underwater forests where thousands of marine animals live.

San Andreas Fault

The San Andreas Fault is a major fracture in Earth's crust where two giant tectonic plates slide next to each other. Many earthquakes occur along this fault.

Douglas fir

The Douglas fir grows in cool, moist forests. Forked bracts stick out between scales on its cones. Birds and other animals eat seeds from the cones.

PACIFIC NORTHWEST

The Pacific Northwest is a diverse region in the northwestern portion of the US. Tall mountains, temperate rainforests, and a pristine coastline provide habitats for many plants and animals.

Volcanic activity

The Pacific Northwest is a very geologically active area. Many of the tall peaks found here are volcanoes. Hot springs are also scattered throughout the region.

Roosevelt elk

The Roosevelt elk are the largest variety of elk in North America. They are named for Theodore Roosevelt, the 26th president of the United States.

Coastal rainforest

Temperate rainforests stretch along the coast of the Pacific Northwest. Evergreen trees rise high in the air. Predators search for prey through masses of ferns on the forest floor.

Bald eagle

Bald eagles are large raptors. Despite their size and majestic appearance, bald eagles have a surprisingly weak call that sounds like a high-pitched squeak!

BALD EAGLES CATCH FISH WITH THEIR TALONS.

Sockeye salmon

Sockeye salmon hatch in freshwater streams but grow up in the ocean. When adults return to the streams to spawn, their heads turn green and their bodies turn bright red.

GINKGO PETRIFIED FOREST STATE PARK

Ginkgo Petrified Forest

Formed millions of years ago, this petrified forest preserves the remains of ancient gingko trees—and more than 50 other species of trees. Petrified wood is the official gem of Washington State.

YELLOWSTONE SUPERVOLCANO

Yellowstone is one of the world's largest active volcanoes. It's a supervolcano. Two massive pools of magma swirl underground. Their heat energizes hot springs, geysers, and other volcanic features on the surface.

DID YOU KNOW?

Yellowstone's supervolcano has had three major eruptions. The last one was 640,000 years ago.

HEAT-LOVING BACTERIA GIVE GRAND PRISMATIC SPRING ITS RAINBOW OF COLORS.

YELLOWSTONE NATIONAL PARK FACTS

Location
Wyoming, Montana, Idaho

Established
March 1, 1872

Size
2,221,766 acres (8,991.16 km²)

Park habitats
Mountain, tundra, grassland, coniferous forest

Hot springs

Yellowstone has many brightly colored hot springs. Grand Prismatic Spring is the largest. Magma heats the water in some hot springs to boiling temperatures.

Geysers

Old Faithful is a geyser. Geysers are hot springs, but the water in them can't flow freely. Pressure builds up until WHOOSH— boiling water shoots high in the sky.

OLD FAITHFUL

GRAND PRISMATIC SPRING

YELLOWSTONE FORESTS

Forests cover over 80 percent of Yellowstone National Park. Some trees, like the Douglas fir, grow up to 100 ft (30 m) tall. The trees provide homes for many animals in the forest.

Forest fires

Wildfires can be dangerous, but they are a natural part of the Yellowstone ecosystem. Some plant species are adapted for fire. Their seeds only open when it's superhot.

Petrified forest

One Yellowstone forest is like no other because its trees are petrified! Fifty million years ago, a volcano erupted. Ash, mud, and debris buried the trees. Eventually, the trees turned to stone.

Alaska blueberry

Birds, mice, and even grizzly bears eat these dark blue berries. Bumblebees pollinate the shrubs, which can grow up to 6.5 ft (2 m) tall.

Chinook salmon

Chinook salmon grow up in the ocean. But when it is time to spawn, they return to the streams where they were born.

CHINOOK SALMON CHANGE COLOR WHEN THEY SPAWN.

ALASKA

Beyond its busy urban centers, Alaska's vast wilderness is home to bears that roam the frozen land and eagles that soar through wide, open skies. It is also a land of extremes, with the highest mountain and the longest coastline in the US.

DID YOU KNOW?

In the Koyukon language, the word "Denali" means "the tall one."

Denali

Denali, the tallest mountain in North America, is so high that its peak is always covered in snow. When air collides with the mountain, it can create its own weather conditions.

Sitka alder

The Sitka alder has gray bark and waxy green leaves. But is it a tree or a shrub? Not everyone agrees!

THIS OCTOPUS HAS BLUE BLOOD AND THREE HEARTS!

Giant Pacific octopus

The giant Pacific octopus is the world's largest octopus. It's also really smart. Using its nine brains, this octopus can unscrew jars and solve puzzles.

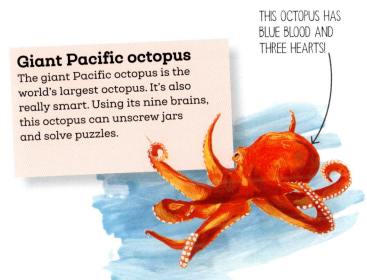

ALASKAN WATERWAYS

State of water

Most of Alaska is surrounded by water. Its coastline is longer than the coastline of all the other 49 states combined! There are also more than 12,000 rivers and three million lakes. That's a lot of water!

IN WINTER, THIS BIRD'S DARKER FEATHERS TURN SNOWY WHITE.

Willow ptarmigan

A male willow ptarmigan puts on a show to catch a mate. He'll waltz, stamp, bow, wag his head, and fan his tail to get her attention.

Grizzly bear

Grizzly bear cubs are born in a winter den. Newborns are blind, hairless, and toothless. They stay with their mothers for two or three years.

Yellow hibiscus

The yellow hibiscus is a native shrub that produces large yellow flowers. Each island in Hawaii has its own official flower, but the yellow hibiscus is the state flower.

THESE FLOWERS OPEN IN LATE AFTERNOON AND CLOSE IN MIDMORNING.

Kilauea

Kilauea sits on the side of Mauna Loa, the largest volcano on Earth. Kilauea is the youngest volcano on Hawaii and the most active volcano on Earth.

HAWAII

Hawaii is a tropical island chain in the middle of the Pacific Ocean. It is filled with rainforests, white sand beaches, and active volcanoes. Many plants and animals found here live nowhere else in the world.

Happy-face spider

This shy, little spider lives on the undersides of leaves. The happy-face pattern varies from spider to spider. It may help protect the spider from birds.

Spectacled parrotfish

Spectacled parrotfish use their toothy beaks to eat coral. They grind the coral into a fine powder. Their poop—a fine white sand—helps build beaches!

Scarlet honeycreeper

Also known as an 'i'iwi, the scarlet honeycreeper's long, curved bill is adapted to drink nectar from long, tubular flowers. The bird's bright red feathers make it easy to spot.

THE SCARLET HONEYCREEPER CAN HOVER IN THE AIR.

Hot spots

The Hawaiian Islands are the tops of gigantic underwater volcanic mountains. The mountains formed as the Pacific Plate moved over a deep plume of lava, called a hot spot, in the Pacific Ocean. The plate is still moving.

DID YOU KNOW?

Hawaii has more endangered species per square mile than anywhere else in the world.

THE HAWAIIAN ISLANDS

THE GIANT MANTA RAY IS ONE OF THE WORLD'S LARGEST FISH.

Giant manta ray

The giant manta ray swims in deep ocean waters with its big mouth wide open. Two specialized flaps funnel water and plankton toward its mouth.

Coral reefs

Hawaii has more than 1,200 miles (1,900 km) of coral reefs. The reefs are made by tiny polyps. They provide food, protection, and a home for ocean animals.

EASTERN AND CENTRAL CANADA

In the eastern and central regions of Canada, whales inhabit the water off the rocky coastline. You may also see puffins nesting on sea cliffs and caribou running through the snow. Two of the world's most amazing water features, Niagara Falls and the Bay of Fundy, are here, too.

ATLANTIC PUFFINS, ATLANTIC COAST

ABOUT EASTERN AND CENTRAL CANADA

About half of Canada's landmass lies within the eastern and central regions. With only a few large cities, there are lots of rural and open spaces for plants and animals to live.

Typical weather

The climate varies considerably in this region. Fog is common in the coastal Maritime provinces, and winters are cold and snowy in the central region.

ON AVERAGE, PRINCE EDWARD ISLAND GETS 114 IN (290 CM) OF SNOW EACH WINTER!

WARM AND COOL OCEAN CURRENTS MEET ALONG CANADA'S EAST COAST. THIS COOLS THE AIR AND CAUSES FREQUENT FOG.

THE MER BLEUE BOG IN ONTARIO PROVIDES A HOME FOR MANY PLANTS AND ANIMALS.

Major landscapes

Stunning mountains line the rocky border along Canada's east coast. But as you move inland, grassy fields, thick forests, and soggy peatlands cover the land.

THE TORNGAT MOUNTAINS LIE ON CANADA'S EASTERN COAST.

Water world

This part of Canada is crisscrossed with rivers flowing out to the Atlantic Ocean. There are also many lakes and a massive inland sea, the Hudson Bay.

FRESH WATER FROM RIVERS AND SALT WATER FROM THE ATLANTIC OCEAN FLOW INTO HUDSON BAY.

THE BAY OF FUNDY HAS THE HIGHEST TIDES IN THE WORLD, AT 49 FT (15 M).

Sites to see

Niagara Falls and the Bay of Fundy are two natural wonders of North America. Both are located in this part of Canada.

NIAGARA FALLS IS ONE OF THE MOST FAMOUS SITES IN NORTH AMERICA.

79

THE BAY OF FUNDY

The Bay of Fundy lies between Nova Scotia and New Brunswick. It is long, narrow, and shaped like a funnel. When the tide rushes in, the water level goes up and up and up!

High tide

For thousands of years, massive tides have swept along the bay's shores. They carved sea stacks, like the Hopewell Rocks. At high tide, only their tops sit above the water.

BAY OF FUNDY FACTS

Highest tide ever recorded
54 ft (16 m)

Number of tides per day
Two high tides and two low tides

Average time between high and low tide
6 hours, 13 minutes

Time for water to travel the full length of the bay and back
About 13 hours

Low tide

At low tide, the water retreats back into the sea. The Hopewell Rocks emerge. You can now see how the powerful tides have sculpted and carved their lower halves.

THE HOPEWELL ROCKS AT LOW TIDE

THE HOPEWELL ROCKS AT HIGH TIDE

THE POWER OF TIDES

A huge amount of water flows in and out of the Bay of Fundy. The water flows swiftly and powerfully. Its regular motion creates interesting features in and around the bay.

Swirling waters

When the tide enters the bay, part of the current pinches off. It forms a whirlpool called Old Sow. Old Sow is as wide as a soccer field, with a 12-ft (3.6-m) drop to its center.

Soupy shores

When the tide retreats, it leaves behind huge stretches of soupy, smelly mud. These mudflats are a favorite place for lots of different kinds of birds.

THE MARITIMES

The Maritime provinces are a group of islands and peninsulas bordered by the Atlantic Ocean in southeastern Canada. Their rocky coasts, deep harbors, and forested interior provide homes to lots of different plants and animals.

Eastern larch
The eastern larch does something most other conifers do not. It loses its needles! In the fall, the tree's blue-green needles turn yellow before falling off.

Common loon
Common loons peer underwater as they swim. When they see prey, they dive deep into the water. They can stay under for almost a minute.

Atlantic walrus
These gigantic mammals are clumsy and slow on land. But in the water, where they search for food on the ocean floor, they're smooth and graceful swimmers.

Singing Sands Beach
At Basin Head on Prince Edward Island, the white silica sand has uniquely rounded grains. When you walk on the sand, it whistles and squeaks!

Eastern red-backed salamander

You'll only find an eastern red-backed salamander in moist places. That's because this salamander has no lungs! It needs the moisture to breathe through its skin.

THIS SALAMANDER HAS A REDDISH-ORANGE STRIPE DOWN ITS BACK.

Atlantic puffin

Atlantic puffins spend most of their time at sea. They come to land to raise chicks in burrows on the sides of grassy sea cliffs.

Alewife

The alewife is an important part of both marine and freshwater ecosystems. Just about everything eats them, including larger fish, seabirds, whales, otters, turtles, and raccoons.

THE MAYFLOWER'S TRUMPET-SHAPED FLOWERS SMELL SPICY AND SWEET.

Mayflower

The mayflower is an evergreen plant that grows as a mat on woodland floors. It is one of the first flowers to bloom in the spring.

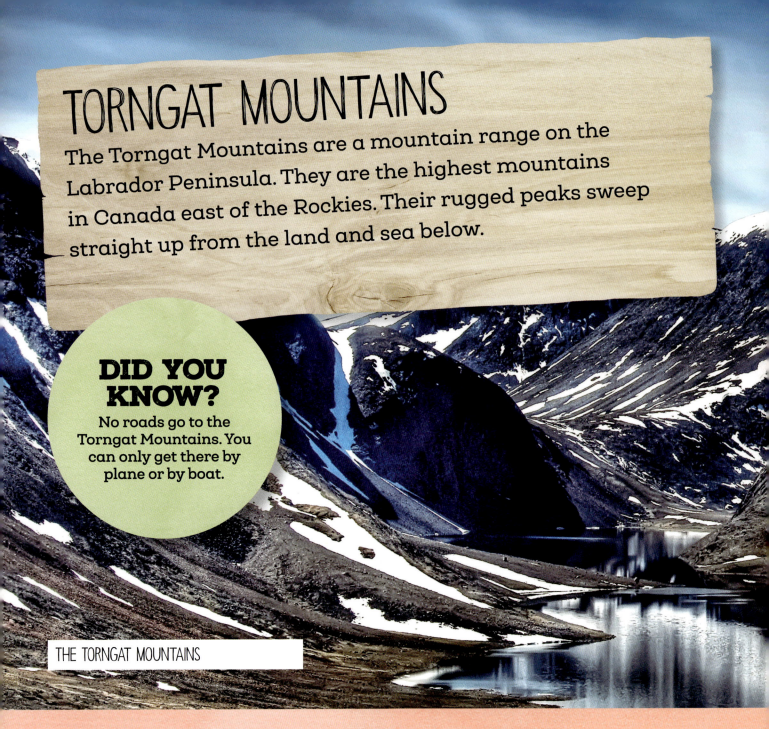

TORNGAT MOUNTAINS

The Torngat Mountains are a mountain range on the Labrador Peninsula. They are the highest mountains in Canada east of the Rockies. Their rugged peaks sweep straight up from the land and sea below.

DID YOU KNOW?

No roads go to the Torngat Mountains. You can only get there by plane or by boat.

THE TORNGAT MOUNTAINS

WATER AND ICE

The Torngat Mountains formed billions of years ago. The area has been shaped by ice. Water and ice are still a big part of the landscape today.

Fjords
When the glaciers receded, water filled the mountain valleys. It created deep blue fjords. They begin on the outer coast and extend into the mountain range.

Rocky valleys

A few million years ago, glaciers slid across the area. They scooped out the U-shaped valleys we see between the rugged peaks today.

TORNGAT'S TREELESS LANDSCAPE

Treeless peaks

You'll find lots of living things in the Torngat Mountains. But one thing you won't find is trees. These jagged peaks lie above the tree line in the Arctic tundra.

Icebergs

During the summer months, massive icebergs float along the coast. The ice in them is about 10,000 years old. Ocean currents carry most of the icebergs down from Greenland.

Melting glaciers

Several small glaciers are still tucked into shaded parts of the Torngats. The ice is thousands of years old. However, global temperatures are rising, and the ice is melting quickly.

ST. LAWRENCE LOWLANDS

The St. Lawrence Lowlands are an area of wetlands, forests, and rolling hills. Split into three parts, they lie along the St. Lawrence River and are bordered by three of the five Great Lakes.

Porcupine
About 30,000 sharp, barbed quills are hidden under a porcupine's soft coat. The quills stand up if the rodent is startled, and they detach when touched.

American beech
Prickly husks surround the American beech tree's fruit. In late summer, the husks split open. Out pop two triangular nuts—a tasty treat for animals and people (but don't eat them in the wild).

THE AMERICAN BLACK DUCK ISN'T BLACK. ITS BODY IS DARK BROWN.

American black duck
American black ducks return to the same marshes each fall. If the marsh is frozen, some American black ducks will starve rather than migrate farther south.

BEAVERS DIG WITH THE SHARP CLAWS ON THEIR FRONT FEET.

Beaver
Beavers slap the water with their tails to warn each other of danger. They also leave their paw prints and scent on mud pies to mark their territory.

Blanding's turtle

Blanding's turtle is easily recognized by its bright yellow throat, neck, and chin. The notched upper jaw makes this turtle look like it's always smiling.

Green-backed heron

This small heron stands quietly on the edge of a wetland. It waits until a small fish, frog, or insect swims by. Then POUNCE! Dinnertime!

A GREEN-BACKED HERON IS ABOUT THE SIZE OF A LARGE CROW.

Five-lined skink

If a predator catches a five-lined skink by its bright blue tail, the tail falls off! The tail thrashes around, distracting the predator, as the skink escapes.

IF A FIVE-LINED SKINK'S TAIL FALLS OFF, IT EVENTUALLY GROWS BACK.

ALTHOUGH FREQUENTLY BLAMED, CANADA GOLDENROD DOES NOT CAUSE HAY FEVER.

Canada goldenrod

Canada goldenrod grows in moist places. You can find it along rivers, roads, and railroads. Bees and butterflies are attracted to its bright yellow flowers.

Conservation

The St. Lawrence Lowlands used to be completely covered in forests and wetlands. Now they are home to two of Canada's largest cities. People here are working to create protected areas for the native wildlife.

MONTREAL, QUEBEC

NIAGARA FALLS

Niagara Falls is truly a sight to behold. Mist rises into the air and the wind whips as water gushes over the falls. More water flows over Niagara Falls than any other waterfall in North America.

DID YOU KNOW?

If you stand in the right spot on a sunny day, you can always see a rainbow in the mist rising above Niagara Falls.

NIAGARA FALLS FACTS

Location
Niagara River, between Ontario, Canada, and New York State, US

Tallest drop
167 ft (51 m)

Maximum width
3,950 ft (1,204 m)

Source
The Great Lakes

The Canadian side

Niagara Falls is actually three separate waterfalls. The larger Horseshoe Falls is the only one in Canada. Ninety percent of the water in Niagara Falls tumbles over Horseshoe Falls.

The US side

American Falls and Bridal Falls are in the US. At one time, there was a cave behind Bridal Falls. The cave collapsed, but you can still see the falls up close.

AMERICAN FALLS AND BRIDAL FALLS

HORSESHOE FALLS

TIME AND CHANGE

Scientists estimate that Niagara Falls formed about 12,000 years ago. The falls are always changing. Some changes are natural and occur over time—others are caused by humans.

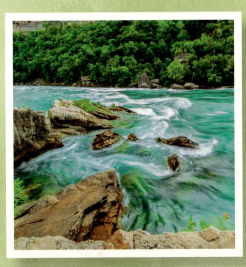

Nature's force

Originally, Niagara Falls was 7 miles (11 km) farther downriver. But erosion ate away at the land and moved the falls to its present site.

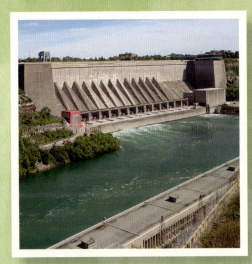

People power

Today, the Canadian and US governments control how much water goes over Niagara Falls. This helps control erosion. Some water is also used to produce hydroelectric power.

HUDSON BAY

Hudson Bay lies in a huge saucer-shaped basin in northeastern Canada. This ocean inlet is nearly landlocked. It flows through straits and channels to join the Arctic and Atlantic oceans on its northern end.

Hudson Bay toad
This is a rare species of toad only found in the Hudson Bay area. The red warts on its body secrete a poisonous milky fluid that protects it from predators.

POLAR BEARS

Wapusk National Park

Manitoba's Wapusk National Park protects one of the polar bears' favorite spots in the world to build dens. In late February, young cubs leave their dens to explore their snowy home—under mom's watchful eye, of course.

CANADA GEESE HONK TO COMMUNICATE WITH EACH OTHER.

DID YOU KNOW?
The Hudson Bay's southeastern shore, a perfect arc, may have been created by a meteorite.

Canada goose
Canada geese fly in V-shaped formations when they migrate. The birds take turns at the front, where it takes more energy to fly into the wind.

Labrador tea
Labrador tea is a shrub that grows in bogs, swamps, and wet conifer forests. Bumblebees pollinate this plant. White-tailed deer and moose sometimes eat it.

ARCTIC TERNS CAN BE VERY AGGRESSIVE WHEN THEIR YOUNG ARE THREATENED.

Arctic tern
Arctic terns have the longest migration of any bird. Each year, they leave their breeding grounds in the Arctic to spend the summer in Antarctica.

Beluga whale
The beluga is a white-toothed whale. In the summer, up to 57,000 belugas go to Hudson Bay estuaries to give birth to their calves.

Arctic fox
During the winter, the Arctic fox sports a thick white coat. When spring arrives, the fox sheds this coat and grows a thinner brown coat of fur.

Sea ice algae
During winter, sea ice algae is frozen in the ice. When the ice melts in spring, the algae becomes food for many animals.

THE FOX'S TAIL MAKES UP ABOUT ONE-THIRD OF ITS TOTAL LENGTH.

CANADIAN SHIELD

The Canadian Shield is a U-shaped piece of continental crust that covers about half of Canada. It is dotted with thousands of small lakes, which formed when glaciers eroded the land during the last ice age.

Peatlands
Peatlands, a type of wetland, cover much of the Canadian Shield. Mosses and woody plants slowly decay, forming layers of peat in the soggy, wet ground.

Boreal owl
Boreal owls watch out for prey from a perch. They have excellent eyesight and hearing. They can even catch prey completely hidden by snow.

THE HARE'S FUR IS BROWN IN THE SUMMER.

Snowshoe hare
Snowshoe hares are small mammals with big feet. Long, thick hairs on the soles of those feet help the hares walk on top of the snow.

Sleeping Giant
Take a close look at this collection of rock formations near Thunder Bay, Ontario. Can you see the giant fast asleep on its back?

Sphagnum moss

Sphagnum moss grows so close together in peatlands that it forms floating mats. The mats are strong enough to hold up the weight of several moose!

Canada lynx

The Canada lynx is a patient nighttime stalker. When its favorite prey, the snowshoe hare, gets close, the lynx leaps to catch its meal.

EXTRA-LARGE FEET HELP THE LYNX TRAVEL OVER DEEP, POWDERY SNOW.

Moose

Moose have the largest and heaviest antlers of any deer. They can grow up to 6 ft (1.8 m) long and weigh up to 80 lb (36 kg).

ANCIENT ROCKS

Earth's oldest rocks

The Canadian Shield contains some of the oldest rocks on Earth. Researchers dated rocks found on the northern shores of Hudson Bay at 4.28 billion years old. Earth is 4.6 billion years old.

MORAINE LAKE, BANFF NATIONAL PARK

WESTERN CANADA

Tall mountains split western Canada into two distinctly different regions. Flat, open prairies lie on one side, and coastal rainforests can be found on the other. The different habitats provide homes for a rich variety of plants and animals. This area also features some of the most spectacular national parks in the country.

Sites to see

Nestled among western Canada's mountains are Banff and Jasper National Parks. The Canadian Badlands are found in the prairies.

ALBERTA'S BADLANDS ARE FILLED WITH INTERESTING ROCK FORMATIONS CALLED HOODOOS.

MELTING GLACIERS HAVE CREATED THE TURQUOISE LAKE MORAINE IN BANFF NATIONAL PARK.

ABOUT WESTERN CANADA

Moving west across Canada, the land flattens dramatically into grand prairies. The grasslands stop abruptly at the Coast Mountains. On the other side of the mountains, temperate rainforests lead to golden beaches along the Pacific Coast.

Important ecosystems

Canada has a wide assortment of ecosystems. In the west, two important and distinctive ecosystems are temperate rainforests and the prairies.

FLAT, OPEN GRASSLANDS STRETCH FOR AS FAR AS YOU CAN SEE IN THE CANADIAN PRAIRIES.

TEMPERATE RAINFORESTS FLOURISH IN BRITISH COLUMBIA ALONG CANADA'S SOUTHWESTERN COAST.

CANADA'S PACIFIC COAST HAS MILD SEASONS. IT IS THE WETTEST PART OF THE COUNTRY.

The water's edge

British Columbia's western edge borders the Pacific Ocean. Many rivers flow from the mountains into low-lying deltas.

MOUNT WADDINGTON IS THE HIGHEST PEAK IN THE COAST RANGE MOUNTAINS, AT 13,186 FT (4,019 M).

Highs and lows

Coastal mountain ranges are found just inland from British Columbia's Pacific Coast. The Okanagan Valley lies between the mountain ranges.

THE OKANAGAN VALLEY IS DRY ENOUGH TO TECHNICALLY BE CALLED A DESERT.

IN EARLY FALL, THESE FLOWERS TURN INTO BRIGHT RED SEED PODS.

Plains hog-nosed snake

This stout-bodied prairie snake has an upturned scale at the tip of its snout. That scale gives the snake its hog-nosed appearance.

Prickly wild rose

The prickly wild rose is a shrub that can grow up to 10 ft (3 m) tall. Thorny stems protect the sweet-smelling pink flowers.

WHEN THREATENED, THIS SNAKE FLARES ITS NECK, HISSES, AND PLAYS DEAD.

THE PRAIRIES

The Prairies lie sandwiched between the forests of Ontario and the peaks of the Rocky Mountains. Flat fields and open skies seem to stretch as far as the eye can see!

DID YOU KNOW?

Temperate grasslands like these are the most endangered ecosystem in the world.

THIS OWL CAN TURN ITS HEAD 180 DEGREES TO LOOK IN ANY DIRECTION.

Great horned owl

These owls aren't afraid to attack some pretty big prey. Sometimes, the results are unfortunate, leaving the owl covered with porcupine quills or reeking of skunk!

Largeheaded grasshopper

The largeheaded grasshopper has a slanted face, short wings, and—you guessed it—a big head. It is a poor flier, which mainly feeds on grasses.

BARN SWALLOWS BATHE, DRINK, AND EVEN FEED THEIR BABIES WHILE FLYING.

Barn swallow

Barn swallows eat all kinds of flying insects. These swift fliers make quick turns and deep dives, since they catch most of their prey in midair.

Blue grama

Blue grama is a grass that grows on dry prairies. It is also called mosquito grass because its seed spikes look like mosquito larvae.

THE CROOKED BUSH

The Crooked Bush

Aspens are normally tall, straight trees. But in this grove in Saskatchewan, the trunks and branches are twisted and bent. There are several theories about why this happened: lightning, a meteorite, or a genetic mutation.

ONE SQUIRREL KEEPS A WATCH OUT FOR DANGER.

Richardson's ground squirrel

Richardson's ground squirrels behave more like prairie dogs than squirrels. They even dig tunnels, creating large colonies underground in the prairie.

THE CANADIAN BADLANDS

Seventy-five million years ago, southern Alberta was a subtropical paradise. It was home to all sorts of dinosaurs. Today, the rocky landscape has eroded into deep canyons and strangely shaped hoodoos.

Canyons

Badlands form where wind and water carve away weak layers of sedimentary rock. The erosion creates deep, narrow canyons, called coulees, with multicolored walls.

HORSESHOE CANYON

Hoodoos

Hoodoos are a product of erosion in the Badlands. Hoodoos are made of soft sandstone, with a harder rock on top. They stand up to 22 ft (7 m) tall.

HOODOOS IN THE CANADIAN BADLANDS

DID YOU KNOW?

If the hard rock on top is removed, a hoodoo will quickly erode.

DINO LAND

Millions of years ago, an asteroid crashed into what is modern-day Mexico. The collision caused rivers in Canada to flood, burying dinosaurs in mud. Today, the Canadian Badlands are a great place to find fossils.

Albertosaurus

Fossil remains of Albertosaurus were discovered in Horseshoe Canyon. This big dinosaur was an early relative of the Tyrannosaurus rex. It was the first meat-eating dino discovered in Canada.

Fossilized nesting site

At Devil's Coulee in the Badlands, a teenage girl discovered Canada's first dinosaur nesting site. It contained fossilized nests, eggs, and embryonic remains of a new species of hadrosaur.

BATS ARE THE ONLY MAMMALS THAT CAN FLY.

Little brown bat

A little brown bat's heart beats more than 1,000 times a minute when it flies, but only 20 times a minute when it hibernates.

BANFF AND JASPER

Step into the Canadian Rockies and you'll find two of Canada's crown jewels: Banff and Jasper National Parks. The parks feature glaciers, waterfalls, and turquoise lakes. You might even see a lynx, bear, or bighorn sheep.

OBSERVE FROM A DISTANCE

Yellow lady's slipper

This orchid can be found from Alaska all the way down to the southern US. Insects enter the shoe-shaped pouch and travel through the flower to collect pollen.

Respecting animals

Lots of animals roam these beautiful national parks. But you should never approach or feed animals in the wild. It's not safe for you or for them. Wild animals can get scared and aggressive toward people. If an animal notices you, back up—you're too close.

MALE ELK GROW A NEW SET OF ANTLERS EACH YEAR.

ELK GRUNT, SQUEAL, BARK, AND WHISTLE TO TALK TO EACH OTHER.

North American elk

Elk are social animals that live in large herds for much of the year. Elk are also called wapiti, a Shawnee word meaning "white rump."

Moraine Lake

Moraine Lake is in Banff National Park. The lake fills a valley surrounded by 10 mountain peaks. Melting glaciers fill it with brilliant blue-green waters.

Canada jay

In cold weather, the Canada jay puffs up its thick, fluffy feathers. The feathers are on its legs, feet, and even in its nostrils!

THE LODGEPOLE PINE'S SHARP, POINTY NEEDLES GROW IN PAIRS.

DID YOU KNOW?

Banff National Park was established in 1885. It is the oldest national park in Canada.

American pika

American pikas live under rocks high up on treeless mountain slopes. They store food in piles called haypiles. In winter, they move haypiles into their dens.

Lodgepole pine

Lodgepole pines store their seeds inside egg-shaped cones. The cones are sealed shut. It takes a wildfire to open the cones so that new plants can grow.

A WOLVERINE HAS DARK, GLOSSY FUR WITH TWO GOLDEN STRIPES DOWN THE BACK.

Wolverine
This mammal is a member of the weasel family. It is about as big as a medium-sized dog, with long, sharp, semi-retractable claws, and a bite strong enough to crush bone.

COAST MOUNTAINS

The Coast Mountains lie on North America's west coast, facing the Pacific Ocean. They begin in British Columbia and run up into Alaska. Dense forests cover their western slopes.

The joker
The joker is a little moth that emerges in early spring. When it gets wet, this bright green moth turns dark yellow.

Skunk cabbage
The beautiful yellow flower that blossoms from this plant in late spring has a not-so-secret way to attract flies for pollination: it has a very stinky smell!

Rubber boa

The rubber boa knows how to confuse predators. Its head looks just like its tail! It even jabs its tail like a striking head when attacked.

THE RUBBER BOA LOOKS AND FEELS LIKE A RUBBER SNAKE!

IN MIDSUMMER, BEARS LOVE TO EAT THIS SHRUB'S BRIGHT RED BERRIES.

Devil's club

This sprawling shrub has a wonderful smell. But don't touch! Its crooked stems and large broad leaves are covered with prickly spines. Ouch!

Clark's nutcracker

Clark's nutcracker has an excellent memory. This mountain bird buries thousands of seeds in the soil. Nine months later, it can find 90 percent of those seeds!

Pacific Ring of Fire

The Coast Mountains are part of the Ring of Fire, a volcanic path along the Pacific Ocean. Tectonic plates–giant pieces of Earth's crust–interact here, creating many volcanoes and earthquakes.

THE WORD "HOARY" MEANS GRAY OR WHITE WITH AGE.

Hoary marmot

This large rodent is about as big as a house cat. When a predator approaches, it sends out an alarm that sounds like a whistle.

PART OF THE RING OF FIRE

THE OKANAGAN VALLEY

The Okanagan Valley is in British Columbia. It lies between the Columbia, Cascade, and Coast mountain ranges. This land of low hills and long, thin lakes is one of the warmest and driest places in Canada.

DID YOU KNOW?

There are 35 provincial parks in the Okanagan Valley region.

OKANAGAN VALLEY FACTS

Location
British Columbia, Canada and Washington State, US

Length
124.5 miles (200 km)

Width
12.8 miles (20 km)

Formed
Between 11,000 and 9,000 years ago

Climate

The Okanagan Valley lies in the rain shadow of the Coast and Cascade mountains. The mountains block most precipitation, giving the valley a desert climate.

Fruit basket of Canada

The Okanagan Valley may be dry, but with help from irrigation, the valley has become a prime area for growing many kinds of fruit.

GRAPES IN A VINEYARD

OSOYOOS DESERT IN THE OKANAGAN AREA

SHAPING THE LANDSCAPE

The Okanagan landscape was created at the end of the last ice age. Retreating glaciers scraped across the land. They left behind a chain of long, thin lakes and other natural features.

Okanagan Lake

Okanagan Lake is the largest lake in the valley. Its beaches are surrounded by ponderosa pines and sagebrush. According to legend, a giant lake monster named Ogopogo lives in its waters.

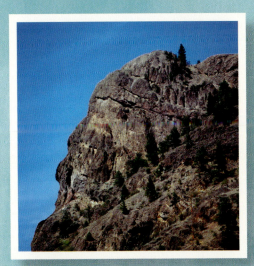

Giant's Head Mountain

Giant's Head Mountain towers above Okanagan Lake. The mountain is an extinct volcanic dome. Glaciers carved the facelike features that give the mountain its name.

Evergreen huckleberry

This slow-growing shrub has red stems. In late summer, its clusters of pink-and-white, bell-shaped flowers turn into dark blue berries.

PACIFIC COAST

Canada's Pacific Coast region includes the western shores of British Columbia. It is an area of low-lying islands, temperate rainforests, and deep fjords. Tall coastal mountain ranges form its eastern border.

Fjords

Fjords are long, deep, narrow bodies of water with steep sides. They reach far inland from the coast. Their water comes from the ocean, rivers, and melting glaciers.

Kermode bear

Kermode bears are a rare subspecies of black bear that has white fur. They live in coastal rainforests on islands off the British Columbia coast.

THESE HORNETS, A KIND OF WASP, ARE PESTS THAT KILL HONEYBEES.

Asian giant hornet

The Asian giant hornet, native to Asia, was discovered in British Columbia in 2019. It is the largest hornet in the world and lives in underground nests.

Orca

Two kinds of orcas live off of Canada's Pacific coast. Resident orcas are fish-eaters that feast on salmon. Transient orcas mainly eat other marine mammals.

Black-footed albatross

These seabirds spend most of their time in the air, but they rarely flap their wings. Instead, they swoop down, ride the wind up, and swoop down again.

DID YOU KNOW?

Orcas are the largest members of the dolphin family.

EACH OF THIS SQUID'S TENTACLES HAS UP TO 200 HOOKED SUCKERS.

SOME WESTERN RED CEDARS ARE MORE THAN A THOUSAND YEARS OLD.

Western red cedar

The western red cedar can grow to about 200 ft (60 m) tall. Its sweet-smelling wood is naturally resistant to decay.

Humboldt squid

This aggressive predator lives in the deep sea. Its nickname is "red devil" because it can turn bright red. Sometimes, the coloring is camouflage, since most deep-sea animals can't see the color red.

CARIBOU, BOREAL ZONE

NORTHERN CANADA

Northern Canada's landscape features
boreal forests, tundra, and snow-covered
islands in the Arctic. Plants and animals that live
here have adapted to survive the chilly climate.
This is the land of the northern lights and the
midnight sun. It may be a cold place, but
it is also a wonderland full of life.

Northern ecosystems

Many plants and animals live in northern Canada. Some are summer visitors. Others have adapted to survive here year-round, despite the extreme living conditions in some parts of the region.

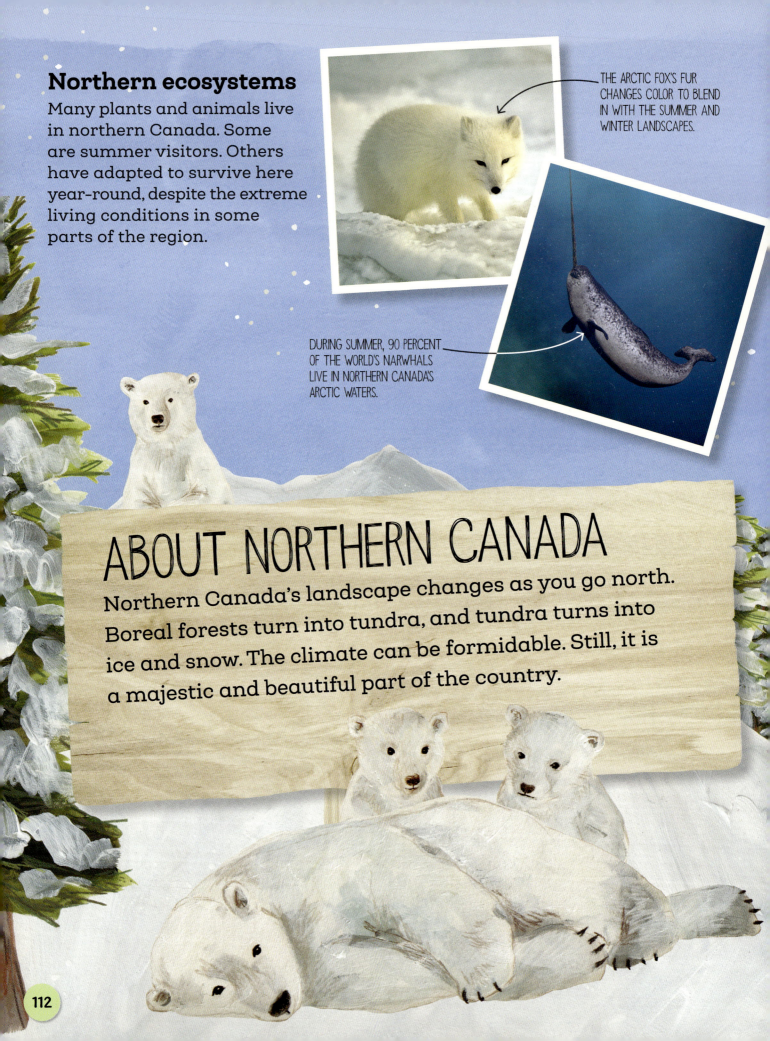

THE ARCTIC FOX'S FUR CHANGES COLOR TO BLEND IN WITH THE SUMMER AND WINTER LANDSCAPES.

DURING SUMMER, 90 PERCENT OF THE WORLD'S NARWHALS LIVE IN NORTHERN CANADA'S ARCTIC WATERS.

ABOUT NORTHERN CANADA

Northern Canada's landscape changes as you go north. Boreal forests turn into tundra, and tundra turns into ice and snow. The climate can be formidable. Still, it is a majestic and beautiful part of the country.

Light show

Because of Earth's tilt, sunlight affects far northern Canada in ways most visibly seen at the poles. This includes 24-hour days, 24-hour nights, and the aurora borealis.

THE AURORA BOREALIS, OR NORTHERN LIGHTS, CREATES A BEAUTIFUL LIGHT SHOW IN THE NIGHT SKY.

DURING THE SUMMER MONTHS, SUNLIGHT SHINES 24 HOURS A DAY IN PARTS OF NORTHERN CANADA.

Frozen lands

Snow and ice cover many parts of the far north. Below that is an area of tundra. Here, plants grow in permafrost during the short summers.

RISING TEMPERATURES ARE CAUSING CANADA'S ICE SHELVES TO BREAK APART.

WARMER TEMPERATURES MAY BE CAUSING MORE LIGHTNING, WHICH SPARKS WILDFIRES IN BOREAL FORESTS.

SNOWFALL IN NORTHERN CANADA IS EXPECTED TO DECREASE FIVE TO 10 PERCENT EACH DECADE BY 2050.

Extreme climate

In northern Canada, blizzards, ice storms, and bone-chilling winds are common. But climate change is altering the landscape here in many ways.

Wood bison
Wood bison graze on grass in meadows between forests. They have longer tails and shorter beards than their cousins, the plains bison. They are also slightly larger.

A TOPCOAT OF HOLLOW HAIRS HELPS TO KEEP A CARIBOU WARM IN COLD TEMPERATURES.

THE BOREAL ZONE

The boreal zone covers just over half of Canada. Most of this region is covered by forests. But there are plenty of wetlands, lakes, mountains, and coastlines, too. Those areas have no trees.

Woodland caribou
Woodland caribou spend summers in boreal forests and winters in the tundra. They use their broad hooves to dig for lichen under the snow.

Great Bear Lake
Great Bear Lake is in the Northwest Territories. It has five deep arms filled with clear water. It is the largest lake completely located within Canada.

Black spruce

This small, narrow evergreen tree is usually found in wetlands. Its shallow root system makes it ideally adapted to survive on permafrost.

TREES THAT ARE 100 TO 200 YEARS OLD PRODUCE THE MOST CONES.

Eastern spruce budworm

The eastern spruce budworm is one of the most destructive forest pests in Canada. Its larvae eat the needles, flowers, and cones of black spruce and other trees.

Mountain bluebird

This beautiful little bird can often be seen hovering low over the ground, searching for a tasty insect. Mountain bluebirds gather in large flocks during winter.

Arctic ground squirrel

These rodents spend up to seven months a year hibernating in burrows. While hibernating, they supercool their bodies and then shiver to warm up again.

EVERYTHING FROM HAWKS TO GRIZZLY BEARS PREY ON THESE SQUIRRELS.

A BOREAL FOREST FIRE

Forest fires

There are many fires in the boreal zone. Forest fires can actually help forests be reborn. Fires open seeds, release nutrients, and open the forest canopy (top layer of trees). Most plants are adapted to survive forest fires.

AURORA BOREALIS

The aurora borealis, or the northern lights, illuminates the skies over the northern parts of Earth. Auroras occur when particles from the sun slam into Earth's upper atmosphere and their energy turns into natural glowing lights.

How does it work?

Tiny particles, too small to see, stream away from the sun. The particles are full of energy when they collide with particles in Earth's atmosphere. They release that energy as light.

AURORA BOREALIS OVER CANADA

AURORA SHAPES

The particles in an aurora travel in the direction of Earth's magnetic field (an invisible force field around the planet). The magnetic field is a band that waves back and forth as it moves. This movement creates auroras with different shapes.

Curtain

Curtains are a common aurora shape. When seen from a distance, they look just like the curtains people hang on windows at home.

Colors

Most auroras are green. But sometimes, when the sun's particles travel deeper into Earth's atmosphere, they glow in a rainbow of colors.

MANY PEOPLE HEAR SIZZLING AND POPPING SOUNDS UNDER THE AURORA.

COLORFUL LIGHTS OVER EARTH

Arc

In the early evening, long thin arcs often stretch from one horizon to another. Arcs can kink, fold, swirl, and even stretch out into multicolored rays.

Corona

Coronas appear when many aurora rays meet at a central point. Coronas are one of the rarest and most impressive kinds of auroras.

THE TUNDRA

The word "tundra" comes from a Finnish word meaning "treeless plain." That's a good description for this region, where only low-growing plants can survive the frozen ground.

Gray wolf
Gray wolves can actually have black, white, light-brown, or gray fur. They are social animals that live and hunt in groups called packs.

AN ARCTIC HARE'S COAT IS GRAYISH-BROWN IN SUMMER AND WHITE IN WINTER.

Arctic hare
When threatened, Arctic hares stand on their hind legs and hop away like a kangaroo. They move quickly, traveling up to 40 mph (60 kph)!

Arctic bumblebee
Arctic bumblebees shiver their large flight muscles to create heat. They trap the heat in their thick coats of hair to stay warm.

Reindeer lichen
Reindeer lichen grows in short mats over much of the tundra. It is a slow-growing plant. Mature clumps of the lichen are about 100 years old.

REINDEER LICHEN IS A FAVORITE FOOD OF REINDEER (CARIBOU).

Pingos
Pingos are cone-shaped hills of ice that grow as water is forced up toward the surface and freezes. The biggest pingo, Ibyuk, is as tall as a 15-story building!

Cloudberry

Cloudberries grow in bogs, moist meadows and forests, and the tundra. The berries are quite tasty, and they're full of vitamin C (but don't eat them in the wild).

Tundra swan

Tundra swans mate for life. The parents raise one brood of babies, called cygnets, each year. The cygnets stay with their parents for about two years.

THE MACKENZIE RIVER DELTA

Permafrost

Permafrost is any ground that stays completely frozen for at least two years. There is permafrost beneath about half of the land in Canada.

LONG, SHAGGY HAIR COVERS A LAYER OF SOFT, DENSE WOOL.

Musk ox

Musk oxen have lived in northern Canada since the last ice age. While they may look like bison or cattle, they're more closely related to sheep and goats.

ELLESMERE ISLAND

Ellesmere Island is the most northern island in the Arctic Archipelago. It is one of the most remote places on Earth. It is an island of tall, rugged mountains and deep fjords. Ice shelves extend its northern coast.

MUSK OXEN AT FRAM FJORD

Island wildlife

Ellesmere Island is a polar desert. Few plants can survive here, but there are many species of bird, as well as land mammals, and even 13 kinds of spiders.

A PLACE OF CHANGE

Climate change is transforming Ellesmere Island. The changes are affecting every living thing that calls the island home. People around the world need to work hard to slow down climate change.

Disappearing habitats

Arctic ice caps are an important habitat for many animals, such as polar bears. As ice caps melt, many animals starve or drown because they are unable to adapt.

Lake Hazen

Lake Hazen is Earth's largest Arctic lake. Despite being surrounded by glaciers, this lake is a pocket of warmth. Summer temperatures can get as high as 68°F (20°C)!

DID YOU KNOW?

Ellesmere Island is the third-largest island in Canada and the 10th-largest island in the world.

LAKE HAZEN ON ELLESMERE ISLAND

Shifting ecosystems

Ecosystems change as temperatures rise. Some animals move north, where it's colder. Others, like the Arctic hare, must adapt in order to survive in the new ecosystem.

Thawing permafrost

When permafrost thaws, it releases greenhouse gases, like methane and carbon dioxide, into the atmosphere. This causes temperatures to rise even further.

ARCTIC ARCHIPELAGO

The Arctic Archipelago is a group of islands—94 major islands and 36,469 smaller ones—that lies just north of mainland Canada. The islands are separated by large channels in the Arctic Ocean.

Greater snow goose
Most adult greater snow geese are white. But a few are blue. They have white faces, dark brown bodies, and pale gray upper wings.

Polar bear
Polar bears are the largest carnivores, or meat eaters, that live on land. Although they look white, they actually have black skin and their hair is clear.

Purple mountain saxifrage
The purple mountain saxifrage is one of the first plants to flower in the Arctic each year. Its lilac-and-magenta, star-shaped flowers stand out against the rocky gray terrain.

Baffin Island
Baffin Island is the largest island in Canada and the fifth-largest island in the world. Parts of the island are covered in ice all year long.

Arctic woolly bear moth caterpillar

It can take seven years for this insect to become a moth. To survive, the caterpillar's body freezes in winter and thaws in summer, so it can eat.

THIS INSECT HAS ANTIFREEZE IN ITS BLOOD AND BODY TISSUES.

Arctic willow

The Arctic willow is a dwarf shrub that can grow for over 200 years. Its stems grow horizontally in layers, forming mats on the frozen ground.

Snowy owl

Rings of stiff feathers around the snowy owl's eyes reflect sound waves into its ears. The owl's excellent hearing helps it find prey under the snow.

THE NARWHAL'S GIANT TUSK IS A LONG, SPIRAL TOOTH!

Narwhal

Narwhals are deep divers and can stay underwater for up to 30 minutes. Afterward, they lie on the surface, breathing deeply, to rebuild oxygen for the next dive.

GLOSSARY

archipelago
Group of islands

bayou
Slow-moving creek or swamp often found in shallow rivers, lakes, or estuaries along the coast

bog
Wet, spongy ground

boreal
Relating to or located in northern or mountainous regions

breach
To leap out of the water

burrow
Hole or tunnel dug by animals for shelter or protection

channel
Narrow body of water that flows between two bodies of land

climate
Weather that is usual for an area over a long period of time

conifer
Evergreen tree with cones and narrow leaves called needles

continental crust
Outer layer of the Earth with land on it

delta
Area of land near the coast where a river breaks up into smaller rivers before entering the sea

ecosystem
Community of living things and their nonliving environment, including the soil, water, and air around them

estuary
Wide part at the end of a river where it flows into the sea

fjord
Long, deep, narrow body of water with steep sides

harbor
Sheltered area in deep water

hibernate
Period of inactivity that some animals go through in the winter

invasive
Species that spreads harmfully and quickly in an ecosystem where it is not native

larva
Insect after it hatches from an egg, but before the adult stage

lichen
Plantlike living thing that is part alga and part fungus

marsh
Low, wet area that is usually overgrown with tall grasses

mature
Fully grown plant or animal

migrate
Move from one region to another

native
Original to an area

peat
Soil in a wet area that is made up of partly decayed plants

peninsula
Piece of land nearly surrounded by water

permafrost
Ground that stays completely frozen for at least two years

secrete
To produce and release a fluid or other substance out of the body

spawn
To deposit or fertilize a large number of eggs

strait
Narrow waterway that connects two bodies of water

subtropical
Regions to the north and south of the tropics

supercontinent
Area of land when all the Earth's continents were joined together; known as Pangaea

temperate
Area or climate with mild temperatures

tributary
Stream that flows into a bigger stream or lake

tundra
Treeless plain in an Arctic region that has a layer of permanently frozen soil beneath the surface

wetlands
Very wet areas of land, such as marshes, bogs, and swamps

STATES, PROVINCES, AND TERRITORIES

The northeastern US

- Connecticut
- Delaware
- Maine
- Maryland
- Massachusetts
- New Hampshire
- New Jersey
- New York
- Pennsylvania
- Rhode Island
- Vermont

The midwestern US

- Illinois
- Indiana
- Iowa
- Kansas
- Michigan
- Minnesota
- Missouri
- Nebraska
- North Dakota
- Ohio
- South Dakota
- Wisconsin

Eastern and central Canada

- New Brunswick
- Newfoundland and Labrador
- Nova Scotia
- Ontario
- Prince Edward Island
- Quebec

The southern US

- Alabama
- Arkansas
- Florida
- Georgia
- Kentucky
- Louisiana
- Mississippi
- Oklahoma
- Tennessee
- Texas
- North Carolina
- South Carolina
- Virginia
- West Virginia

The western US

- Alaska
- Arizona
- California
- Colorado
- Hawaii
- Idaho
- Montana
- Nevada
- New Mexico
- Oregon
- Utah
- Washington
- Wyoming

Western Canada

- Alberta
- British Columbia
- Manitoba
- Saskatchewan

Northern Canada

- Northwest Territories
- Nunavut
- Yukon

INDEX

A

Acadia National Park 16–17
Adirondack Mountains 12, 18–19
Agassiz, Lake 48
Alaska 57, 58, 72–3
albatrosses 109
Albertosaurus 101
alders, sitka 73
alewives 83
algae 91
alligators 4, 25, 27, 38
American Falls 89
Appalachian Mountains 25, 27, 28–9
Arctic Archipelago 111, 120, 122–3
armadillos 36
aspens 99
Assateague Island 13, 21
aurora borealis (northern lights) 111, 113, 116–17

B

Badlands, Canadian 96, 100–1
Badlands, South Dakota 53
Badwater Basin 58
Baffin Island 122
Banff National Park 96, 102–3
bass, largemouth 50
bats, little brown 102
bayous 25, 26, 36
bears 4, 28, 73, 90, 108, 120, 122
beavers 86
beeches, American 86
Big Spring 50
bison 42, 53, 55, 114
Black Elk Peak 53
Black Hills 43, 52–3
black-eyed Susans 55
bluebells, Virginia 21
blueberries, Alaska 72
bluebirds, mountain 115
boas, rubber 105
bobcats 33

boreal zone 113, 114–15
Bridal Falls 89
Bubble Rock 17
budworms 115
bumblebees, Arctic 118
buntings, indigo 28
butterflies 44

C

Cadillac Mountain 16
Canadian Shield 44, 92–3
canyons 62–3, 100
carbon dioxide 121
caribou 76, 110–11, 114
caterpillars 123
caves 27, 30–1, 47, 51
cedars, western red 109
Central Lowland 48–9
Chapel Rock 47
Chesapeake Bay 13, 22–3
chipmunks, eastern 19
climate 27, 58, 78, 106, 113
climate change 85, 113, 120, 121
cloudberries 119
Coast Mountains 96, 97, 104–5, 106
Coastal California 66–7
Colorado River 62
condors, California 67
conservation 87
Continental Divide 61
coral reefs 75
coyotes 50
crabs 11, 21, 22, 37
cranberries 13
cranes, sandhill 43
creosote bushes 65
crocodiles 27

D

Death Valley 65
deer, white-tailed 49
Denali 5, 58, 72
devil's clubs 105
Devils Tower 52
dinosaurs 101
dolphins 36–7, 109
Downeast 16–17
ducks 45, 86

E

eagles, bald 69
earthquakes 58, 59, 67
ecosystems 13, 26, 59, 60, 97, 98, 112, 121
eels, American 20
elks 68, 102
Ellesmere Island 120–1
Erie, Lake 46
erosion 100, 101
Everglades 26, 27, 38–9

F

falcons, peregrine 61
fall foliage 11, 12, 13, 19
ferns, cinnamon 19
ferrets, black-footed 55
firs, Douglas 68
fjords 84, 108, 120
floods 35, 63
forest fires 71, 113, 115
fossils 101
foxes 20, 44, 65, 91, 112
frogs 18, 33, 45
fruit 107
Fundy, Bay of 76, 79, 80–1

G

geese 90, 122
geysers 71
Giant's Head Mountain 107
Gila monsters 65
Gingko Petrified Forest 69
glaciers 44, 85, 92, 96, 107, 121
goldenrod, Canada 87
grama, blue 99
Grand Canyon 57, 59, 62–3
Grand Prismatic Spring 59, 70–1
grasses 55
grasshoppers 99
Great Bear Lake 114
Great Lakes 41, 42, 43, 46–7
Great Plains 42, 54–5
Green River Valley 31

Gulf Coast 36–7
gulls, herring 15

H

habitat loss 120
hares 92, 118, 121
Havasu Falls 63
Hawaii 57, 59, 74–5
Hazen, Lake 120–1
hellbenders, Ozark 51
hemlock, eastern 21
herons 36, 87
hibiscus, yellow 74
hickories, shagbark 29
honeycreepers, scarlet 75
hoodoos 96, 100, 101
Hopewell Rocks 80–1
hornets, Asian giant 108
horses, wild 11, 13, 21
Horseshoe Canyon 100–1
Horseshoe Falls 88–9
hot spots 75
hot springs 59, 70–1
Hudson Bay 79, 90–1, 93
hummingbirds 37
Huron, Lake 46
hurricanes 27, 37
hydroelectric power 89

I

ice age 92, 107
ice caves 47
icebergs 85
Indigenous peoples 52
invasive species 39

J

Jasper National Park 96, 102–3
jays, Canada 103
jellyfish, freshwater 50
jokers 104
Joshua trees 64

K

karst topography 51
kelp, giant 67
kettles 18
Kilauea 74

L

lady's slippers, yellow 102
larches, eastern 82
laurels, mountain 29
lenticular clouds 60
levees 35
lichen, reindeer 118
lighthouses 17
lions, mountain 60–1
lizards, Texas horned 54
lobsters 15, 16
loons, common 82
Lowcountry, South
    Carolina 32–3
lynxes, Canada 93

M

magnolias, southern 37
mallards 45
Mammoth Cave 27, 30–1
manatees 39
mangroves, red 38
maple syrup 13, 14
Maritime provinces 82–3
marmots, hoary 105
martens, American 18
mayflowers 83
Mer Bleue Bog 79
Michigan, Lake 46, 47
Mid-Atlantic 20–1
midnight sun 111
migrations 15, 44, 47
Mississippi Flyway 47
Mississippi River 27,
    34–5, 42, 43
Missouri River 34
moccasins, water 51
Mojave Desert 64–5
moose 93
Moraine Lake 94–5, 96,
    103
morels, common 48
moss 32, 93
moths 18, 104, 123
mudflats 81
musk oxen 119, 120
muskrats 48

N

narwhals 112, 123
New England 14–15

newt salamanders,
    eastern 15
Niagara Falls 76, 79, 88–9
nutcrackers, Clark's 105

O

oaks 32, 51
octopuses, giant Pacific
    73
Ohio River 34
Okanagan Lake 107
Okanagan Valley 97,
    106–7
Old Faithful 71
Ontario, Lake 46
orcas 109
owls 44, 92, 98, 123
oystercatchers,
    American 33
Ozarks 41, 42, 50–1

P

Pacific Coast 97, 108–9
Pacific Northwest 57,
    68–9
palmettos 33
panthers, Florida 26, 39
parrotfish, spectacled 74
peatlands 92
permafrost 112, 113, 119,
    121
petrified forests 69, 71
Pictured Rocks 46
pikas, American 103
pin cherries 19
pines 45, 53, 61, 103
pingos 118
polar bears 4, 90, 120,
    122
pollution 23
porcupines 86
prairie dogs 54
prairies 95, 96, 97
Prairies, Canadian
    98–99
pronghorns 54
ptarmigans, willow 73
puffins 83
pupfish, Devils Hole 65
pythons, Burmese 39

R

rabbits, marsh 38
raccoons, common 44
rainforests 68, 95, 96, 97
rays, giant manta 75
redwoods 4, 66
Ring of Fire 59, 105
roadrunners, greater 64
robins, American 21
Rocky Mountains 57,
    60–1
roses, prickly wild 98

S

St. Lawrence Lowlands
    86–7
salamanders 11, 15, 29,
    51, 83
salmon 69, 72
San Andreas Fault 67
sarsaparilla, wild 45
saxifrage, purple
    mountain 122
scorpions 64
sea anemones, green 67
sea ice 91
sea islands 33
sea lions, California 67
sea otters 66
seagulls 46–7
sheep, bighorn 59, 60
Singing Sands Beach 82
skinks, five-lined 87
skunk cabbages 104
skunks, striped 51
snakes 39, 51, 65, 98, 105

T

tarantulas 65
tea, Labrador 91
tectonic plates 67, 105
terns, Arctic 91
Thunder Hole 17
tides 79, 80, 81

toads 60, 90
tornadoes 41, 43
Torngat Mountains 79,
    84–5
tundra 85, 111, 112, 113,
    118–19
turkeys, wild 48
turtles 32, 44, 49, 87

V

violets, common blue 49
volcanoes 57, 58, 59, 68,
    70–1, 74–5, 105

W

Waddington, Mount 97
walruses, Atlantic 82
Wapusk National Park
    90
warblers 19
Washington, Mount 13,
    14
whales 13, 15, 66, 76, 91
whirlpools 81
willows, Arctic 123
Wisconsin Dells 49
wolverines 104
wolves, gray 118
woodchucks 21

Y

Yellowstone National
    Park 57, 59, 70–1

ACKNOWLEDGMENTS

Dorling Kindersley would like to thank the following people for their assistance in the preparation of this book: Jacqueline Hornberger and Margaret Parrish for proofreading; Helen Peters for the index; Sif Nørskov for jacket support; and Srijani Ganguly for additional editorial support.

The publisher would like to thank the following for their kind permission to reproduce their images: (Key: a-above; b-below/bottom; c-center; f-far; l-left; r-right; t-top)

1 Getty Images / iStock: Gerald Corsi / E+. **2 Dreamstime.com:** Melinda Fawver (x3/l); Natakuzmina (br). **3 Alamy Stock Photo:** B Christopher (tl). **Dreamstime.com:** Steve Boyko (br); Joshua Gagnon (ftl); Czuber (ftr); Cheryl Fleishman (crb). **Shutterstock.com:** Miroslav Milda (x2/br); Brian A Wolf (tr). **4 Getty Images / iStock:** Dmitr1ch (t). **4–5 Getty Images:** Sherry Epley / 500px (t). **5 Dreamstime.com:** Matthieuclouis (tc). **Getty Images / iStock:** fstop123 / E+ (c). **Shutterstock.com:** valiant.skies (cra). **6 Dorling Kindersley:** Abby Cook (x5); Abby Cook (tl). **6–7 Getty Images / iStock:** bergserg / DigitalVision Vectors. **7 Dorling Kindersley:** Abby Cook (x6). **Getty Images / iStock:** bergserg / DigitalVision Vectors (br). **8–9 Dreamstime.com:** Anastasiia Malinich (t); Tihomir Trifonov. **8 Alamy Stock Photo:** Tom Reichner (bc); Marian Turcan (bl). **Dorling Kindersley:** Abby Cook (ca); Abby Cook (c); Abby Cook (cr/Leaf). **Getty Images / iStock:** KeithBriley (cl). **Shutterstock.com:** Engel Ching (cr); Quang Ho (crb); Miroslav Milda (cra). **9 Alamy Stock Photo:** Don Johnston_MA (crb). **AWL Images:** ClickAlps (clb). **Dorling Kindersley:** Abby Cook (tr); Abby Cook (bl); Abby Cook (br). **Dreamstime.com:** Gerald Deboer (cr); Anastasiia Malinich (tc); Stephen Moehle (cla); Brent Flint (cb). **SuperStock:** Don Johnston / All Canada Photos (cra). **10–11 Shutterstock.com:** Engel Ching. **11 Dorling Kindersley:** Abby Cook (x2/cla); Abby Cook (cra); Abby Cook (crb). **Getty Images / iStock:** Dmitr1ch (c). **12 Dorling Kindersley:** Abby Cook (x3/t); Abby Cook (br). **Dreamstime.com:** Anna Lisa Yoder (tc). **Getty Images / iStock:** Dmitr1ch (x2/b). **Shutterstock.com:** Andy Williams photos (cra). **13 Alamy Stock Photo:** canadabrian (cra); Simon Crumpton (tc). **Getty Images / iStock:** Aschen (br); HABesen (c). **Getty Images:** Marc Sadowski / EyeEm (bc). **14 Dorling Kindersley:** Abby Cook. **Getty Images / iStock:** DenisTangneyJr (tr). **15 Dorling Kindersley:** Abby Cook (bl); Abby Cook (br). **Dreamstime.com:** Jeffrey Holcombe (tr); Isselee (tl). **16 Alamy Stock Photo:** Fred Bavendam / Minden Pictures (cl). **Getty Images / iStock:** Dmitr1ch (t). **Shutterstock.com:** Winston Tan (bc). **16–17 Dreamstime.com:** Alwoodphoto (t). **17 Dreamstime.com:** Mihai Andritoiu (bl); Sayran (br). **18 Dorling Kindersley:** Abby Cook (cl). **Dreamstime.com:** Gerald Deboer (cra); David Havel (crb). **Getty Images:** Matt Champlin / Moment (b). **18–19 Dreamstime.com:** Tihomir Trifonov. **19 Alamy Stock Photo:** Don Johnston_PL (clb). **Dorling Kindersley:** Abby Cook (cl). **Dreamstime.com:** Anatoly Kazakov (bc); Paul Reeves (tl); Brian Lasenby (crb). **Shutterstock.com:** Sharan Singh (tr). **20 Alamy Stock Photo:** Michael Wood / Stocktrek Images (tl). **Dorling Kindersley:** Abby Cook (cra). **Dreamstime.com:** Jim Cumming (b); Melinda Fawver (cla). **Shutterstock.com:** Miroslav Milda (x5/l). **20–21 Dreamstime.com:** Melinda Fawver (t); Tihomir Trifonov. **21 Depositphotos Inc:** graphicphoto (ca). **Dorling Kindersley:** Abby Cook (br). **Dreamstime.com:** Vrabelpeter1 (clb). **Courtesy of National Park Service**, Lewis and Clark National Historic Trail (tr). **22 Getty Images / iStock:** Dmitr1ch (t); molefranz (bl). **22–23 Getty Images / iStock:** drnadig. **23 Dreamstime.com:** Chernetskaya (cra); Picsfive (tc). **Shutterstock.com:** Jack Looney photography (crb). **24–25 Getty Images / iStock:** KeithBriley. **25 Dorling Kindersley:** Abby Cook (tr). **26 Dorling Kindersley:** Abby Cook. **Dreamstime.com:** John Twynam (cb). **Getty Images:** Jena Ardell / Moment (bc). **27 Alamy Stock Photo:** Pat & Chuck Blackley (clb); Adam Jones / Danita Delimont, Agent (tl). **Dorling Kindersley:** Abby Cook (x3/r); Abby Cook (x3/b). **Dreamstime.com:** C5Media (tc); Romrodinka (bc). **Getty Images:** Warren Faidley / The Image Bank (cr). **28 Alamy Stock Photo:** Stephen J. Krasemann / All Canada Photos (b). **Dorling Kindersley:** Abby Cook (tl). **Dreamstime.com:** Cheryl Fleishman (tr); Tom Meaker (x2/t). **28–29 Dreamstime.com:** Mikhail Makarov (x3); Tihomir Trifonov. **29 Alamy Stock Photo:** George Grall (bl). **Dorling Kindersley:** Abby Cook (ca). **Dreamstime.com:** Tom Meaker (cla). **Getty Images / iStock:** DNY59 (b). **30 Dreamstime.com:** Picsfive (bl). **Getty Images / iStock:** Dmitr1ch (t). **30–31 Courtesy of National Park Service**, Lewis and Clark National Historic Trail. **31 Dreamstime.com:** Julie Feinstein (crb). Courtesy of National Park Service, Lewis and Clark National Historic Trail. **32 Alamy Stock Photo:** Pat Canova (tl). **Dorling Kindersley:** Abby Cook (bl). **32–33 Dreamstime.com:** Tihomir Trifonov. **33 4Corners:** Werner Bertsch (cl). **Alamy Stock Photo:** Robert Read (tl); James Hager / robertharding (bl). **Dorling Kindersley:** Abby Cook (cb). **Dreamstime.com:** Forestpath (r). **34 Dreamstime.com:** Picsfive (bl). **Getty Images / iStock:** Dmitr1ch (t). **34–35 Dreamstime.com:** Sean Pavone. **35 Alamy Stock Photo:** photo.eccles (crb). **Dreamstime.com:** Chris Boswell (cra). **Shutterstock.com:** lavizzara (ca). **36 Alamy Stock Photo:** Hildegard Williams (bl). **Dorling Kindersley:** Abby Cook (c). **Dreamstime.com:** Sander Meertins (tr). **36–37 Alamy Stock Photo:** blickwinkel / Woike (b). **Dreamstime.com:** Tihomir Trifonov. **37 Dorling Kindersley:** Abby Cook (t). **Dreamstime.com:** Natakuzmina (cla); Zenobillis (cr). **Shutterstock.com:** Brian A Wolf (cra). **38 Alamy Stock Photo:** Ethan Welty / Aurora Photos / Cavan Images (bl). **Dorling Kindersley:** Abby Cook (cra); Jerry Young (c). **Dreamstime.com:** Smitty411 (br). **39 Alamy Stock Photo:** NPS Photo (tl); Mansell, Barry / SuperStock (cra). **Dorling Kindersley:** Abby Cook (b). **40–41 Alamy Stock Photo:** Tom Reichner. **41 Dorling Kindersley:** Abby Cook (x2). **42 Dorling Kindersley:** Abby Cook (x3/t); Abby Cook (b). **Dreamstime.com:** Patricia Cale (tc). **Getty Images:** Joanna McCarthy / The Image Bank (ca). **43 Dorling Kindersley:** Abby Cook (crb). **Getty Images:** (bc); Ed Reschke / Stone (tr); Dennis Macdonald / Photographer's Choice RF (cra); **Visions of America / UIG / Collection Mix:** Subjects (c). **Getty Images / iStock:** Kyle Kempf (cl). **44 Dreamstime.com:** Leerobin (br). **Getty Images / iStock:** GlobalP (clb). **Shutterstock.com:** Natalia Kuzmina (tl). **44–45 Dreamstime.com:** Tihomir Trifonov. **45 Dorling Kindersley:** Abby Cook (crb). **Dreamstime.com:** Natallia Khlapushyna (tr); Steven Oehlenschlager (tc); Michiel De Wit (cla); Holly Kuchera (b). **46 Alamy Stock Photo:** aaron peterson.net (cl). **Dreamstime.com:** Dean Pennala (bc). **Getty Images / iStock:** Dmitr1ch (t). **46–47 Dreamstime.com:** Karel Bock. **47 Dreamstime.com:** Ginalaforest (br). **Shutterstock.com:** John McCormick (bl). **48 Alamy Stock Photo:** Chuck Haney / Danita Delimont, Agent (cl). **Dorling Kindersley:** Abby Cook (tl). **Dreamstime.com:** Sergey Uryadnikov (c). **Shutterstock.com:** Tory Kallman (br). **48–49 Dreamstime.com:** Tihomir Trifonov. **49 Alamy Stock Photo:** B Christopher (crb). **Dorling Kindersley:** Abby Cook (clb). **Dreamstime.com:** Jim Cumming (t); Joshua Gagnon (cb). **Shutterstock.com:** Lorraine Swanson (br). **50 Alamy Stock Photo:** John Pitcher / agefotostock (b). **Dorling Kindersley:** Abby Cook (cra). **Dreamstime.com:** Melinda Fawver (x2/l). **Getty Images:** John Elk III (tl). **50–51 Dreamstime.com:** Tihomir Trifonov. **51 Alamy Stock Photo:** Clint Farlinger (cr). **Dorling Kindersley:** Abby Cook (bl). **Dreamstime.com:** Iulian Gherghel (tl); Isselee (cl). **52 Dreamstime.com:** Kevin Walker (bc). **Getty Images / iStock:** Dmitr1ch (t). **52–53 Shutterstock.com:** Wollertz. **53 Alamy Stock Photo:** Images By T.O.K. (cra). **naturepl.com:** Charlie Summers (bl). **Shutterstock.com:** Randy Runtsch (br). **54 Alamy Stock Photo:** Ivan Kuzmin (cr). **Dorling Kindersley:** Abby Cook (cl). **Dreamstime.com:** Designpicssub / Design Pics / Jack Goldfarb (br); Marek Uliasz (clb). **Shutterstock.com:** Quang Ho (x2/l). **55 Alamy Stock Photo:** SBS Eclectic Images (cla); Marian Turcan (x2/tc). **Dorling Kindersley:** Abby Cook (b). **Getty Images / iStock:** CarbonBrain (tr). **Shutterstock.com:** Quang Ho (tr/Flower). **56–57 Dreamstime.com:** Stephen Moehle. **57 Dorling Kindersley:** Abby Cook (x3). **Getty Images / iStock:** Dmitr1ch (c). **58 Dorling Kindersley:** Abby Cook (x2/t); Abby Cook (b). **Dreamstime.com:** David Hayes (cra); Nouseforname (tc). **Getty Images / iStock:** Dmitr1ch (x2/b/Board). **59 Alamy Stock Photo:** World History Archive (cr). **Dreamstime.com:** Larry Gevert (tc); MNStudio (clb). **Shutterstock.com:** Lorcel (bc); MH Anderson Photography (cla). **60 Alamy Stock Photo:** James Hager / robertharding (c). **Dorling Kindersley:** Abby Cook (tl). **60–61 Dreamstime.com:** Tihomir Trifonov. **61 Dorling Kindersley:** Abby Cook (r). **Dreamstime.com:** Ashley Werter (cl). **62 Dreamstime.com:** Picsfive (bl). **Getty Images / iStock:** Dmitr1ch (t). **62–63 Dreamstime.com:** John Sirlin. **63 Dreamstime.com:** Granitepeaker (cra). **Getty Images / iStock:** MasterLu (c). **Shutterstock.com:** Mike Buchheit (crb). **64 123RF.com:** Natalie Ruffing (br/x2). **Alamy Stock Photo:** Glenn Bartley / All Canada Photos (tl). **Dorling Kindersley:** Abby Cook (clb). **65 Alamy Stock Photo:** Stone Nature Photography (clb). **Dorling Kindersley:** Abby Cook (cla). **Dreamstime.com:** Isselee (br); Oliclimb (cr). **Getty Images / iStock:** Gerald Corsi (t). **66 Alamy Stock Photo:** Claudio Contreras / Nature Picture Library (tr); Suzi Eszterhas / Nature Picture Library (br). **Dorling Kindersley:** Abby Cook (l). **67 Alamy Stock Photo:** Blue Planet Archive PCO (br); Brandon Cole Marine Photography (tl); Lee Rentz (tr). **Dorling Kindersley:** Abby Cook (cl). **Getty Images:** Lloyd Cluff / Corbis Documentary (bl). **68 Depositphotos Inc:** CoreyFord (tl). **Dorling Kindersley:** Abby Cook (bl). **Dreamstime.com:** Anastasiia Malinich (tr). **68–69 Alamy Stock Photo:** Mike Grandmaison / All Canada Photos (b). **Dreamstime.com:** Tihomir Trifonov. **69 Alamy Stock Photo:** Westend61 GmbH (cra). **Depositphotos Inc:** zrfphoto (cr). **70 Dreamstime.com:** Picsfive (bl). **Getty Images / iStock:** Dmitr1ch (t). **70–71 Dreamstime.com:** Gert Hochmuth. **71 Alamy Stock Photo:** USFS Photo (cra). **Dreamstime.com:** Timothy Stirling (crb); Brett Taylor (ca). **72 Alamy Stock Photo:** Tom Walker (tl). **Dorling Kindersley:** Abby Cook (cra). **Dreamstime.com:** Steve Allen (b). **72–73 Alamy Stock Photo:** blickwinkel / S. Derder (t). **Dreamstime.com:** Tihomir Trifonov. **73 Dorling Kindersley:** Abby Cook (cla); Robert Royse (clb). **Getty Images / iStock:** Gerald Corsi / E+ (b). **74 Alamy Stock Photo:** Phil Degginger (tr); Tami Kauakea Winston / Photo Resource Hawaii (ca). **Dorling Kindersley:** Abby Cook (cr). **Getty Images / iStock:** Olga Skripnik (tl). **74–75 Dorling Kindersley:** Abby Cook (b). **75 Alamy Stock Photo:** Planet Observer / UIG (cr). **Getty Images:** Todd Aki / Moment Open (cb). **Shutterstock.com:** Thomas Chlebecek (ca). **76 Dorling Kindersley:** Abby Cook (x2). **Getty Images / iStock:** Dmitr1ch (c). **76–77 SuperStock:** Don Johnston / All Canada Photos. **78 Alamy Stock Photo:** Barrett & MacKay / All Canada Photos (cb). **Dorling Kindersley:** Abby Cook; Abby Cook (x2/t). **Shutterstock.com:** Rob Crandall (br). **79 Alamy Stock Photo:** All Canada Photos (tc); Aussiemandias (cla). **Dorling Kindersley:** Abby Cook (tr); Abby Cook (x3/b). **Dreamstime.com:** Lequint (bc); Christoph Lischetzki (clb). **Getty Images / iStock:** pkline (cr). **80–81 Alamy Stock Photo:** Graca Victoria. **80 Dreamstime.com:** Picsfive (bl). **Getty Images / iStock:** Dmitr1ch (t). **81 Alamy Stock Photo:** Robert Bird (cra). **Dreamstime.com:** Paul Brady (ca). **Shutterstock.com:** vagabond54 (crb). **82 Dorling Kindersley:** Abby Cook (c). **Dreamstime.com:** Vladimir Melnik (bl). **Getty Images:** Danielle Donders / Moment (crb). **82–83 Dreamstime.com:** Tihomir Trifonov. **83 Alamy Stock Photo:** Milton Cogheil (cl). **Dreamstime.com:** Jeffrey Holcombe (x2/bl); Michiel De Wit (cla). **84 Alamy Stock Photo:** Egmont Strigl / agefotostock (bc). **Getty Images / iStock:** Dmitr1ch (t). **SuperStock:** John Sylvester (bl). **84–85 Alamy Stock Photo:** All Canada Photos (t). **85 Alamy Stock Photo:** Fabrice Simon / Biosphoto (tr). Parks Canada: (br). **86 Dorling Kindersley:** Abby Cook (cl). **Dreamstime.com:** Jnjhuz (bl); Tihomir Trifonov (tr); Paul Reeves (cr). **86–87 Dreamstime.com:** Tihomir Trifonov. **87 Dorling Kindersley:** Abby Cook (tl). **Dreamstime.com:** Gerald Deboer (cl); Donyanedomam (tr); Kazakovmaksim (cr); Rodrigolab (br). **88 Dreamstime.com:** Picsfive (bl). **Getty Images / iStock:** Dmitr1ch (t). **88–89 Getty Images / iStock:** Starcevic / E+. **89 Dreamstime.com:** Linda Harms (ca); Vitaldrum (cra). **Shutterstock.com:** Elena Berd (crb). **90 Alamy Stock Photo:** Andr Gilden (cl). **Dorling Kindersley:** Abby Cook (tl). **Dreamstime.com:** Wrangel (bc). **90–91 Dreamstime.com:** Tihomir Trifonov. **91 Alamy Stock Photo:** E.R. Degginger (tr). **Dorling Kindersley:** Abby Cook (tl). **Dreamstime.com:** Hakoar (cla); John jJ Henderson / Visceralimage (br). **Getty Images:** Jason Edwards / The Image Bank (clb). **92 Alamy Stock Photo:** Design Pics (tr). **Dorling Kindersley:** Abby Cook (clb). **Dreamstime.com:** Jim Cumming (crb). **92–93 Dreamstime.com:** Johnsroad7 (b); Tihomir Trifonov. **93 Dorling Kindersley:** Abby Cook (tr). **Dreamstime.com:** Antonina Germanova (cla). **Getty Images / iStock:** BirdImages / E+ (cl). **Jonathan ONeil:** (cr). **94–95 AWL Images:** ClickAlps. **95 Dorling Kindersley:** Abby Cook (x2). **Getty Images / iStock:** Dmitr1ch (c). **96 Dorling Kindersley:** Abby Cook (b). **Dreamstime.com:** Lubomir Chudoba (ca); Tomas Nevesely (tl). **Getty Images / iStock:** Dmitr1ch (x2/b). **97 Alamy Stock Photo:** Chris Cheadle (bc). **Dorling Kindersley:** Abby Cook (ca). **Dreamstime.com:** Prathan Keawkhum (c); Sara Winter (tc); Nalidsa Sukprasert (crb). **Shutterstock.com:** Nancy Anderson (cra). **98 Dreamstime.com:** Cynoclub (tl); Jan Kamierczak (tl/Rose); Isselee (bl). **98–99 Dorling Kindersley:** Abby Cook (b). **Dreamstime.com:** Tihomir Trifonov. **99 Dorling Kindersley:** Abby Cook (tc). **Dreamstime.com:** Jason Yoder (tr). **100 Getty Images / iStock:** Dmitr1ch (t). **100–101 Alamy Stock Photo:** David Wall. **101 Alamy Stock Photo:** Judy Waytiuk (crb). **Dreamstime.com:** Steve Boyko (ca). **Getty Images / iStock:** leonello (cra). **102 Alamy Stock Photo:** Michael Durham / Nature Picture Library (tl). **Dorling Kindersley:** Abby Cook (c). **Dreamstime.com:** Helena Bilkova (cl). **102–103 Dreamstime.com:** Tihomir Trifonov; Sakalouski Uladzislau (b). **103 Dreamstime.com:** Hpbfotos (r). **104–105 Dreamstime.com:** Tihomir Trifonov. **104 Alamy Stock Photo:** Jeff Lepore (cr). **Dorling Kindersley:** Abby Cook (br). **Dreamstime.com:** Vladislav Jirousek (t). **105 Dorling Kindersley:** Abby Cook (cl). **Dreamstime.com:** Czuber (tr); Yarr65 (br). **Getty Images / iStock:** BirdImages (bl). **106 Dreamstime.com:** Picsfive (bl). **Getty Images / iStock:** Dmitr1ch (t). **106–107 Alamy Stock Photo:** Douglas Lander. **107 Alamy Stock Photo:** Gunter Marx / OK (crb). **Dreamstime.com:** Davidrh (cra); Vismax (ca). **108 Alamy Stock Photo:** John Zada (cra). **Dorling Kindersley:** Abby Cook (crb). **Dreamstime.com:** Brent Flint (tr); Pkzphotos (tl). **Getty Images / iStock:** KenCanning / E+ (bl). **108–109 Dreamstime.com:** Tihomir Trifonov. **109 Alamy Stock Photo:** Nature Picture Library (clb). **Dorling Kindersley:** Abby Cook (tl). **Dreamstime.com:** Marilyn Barbone (crb); Slowmotiongli (tr). **110–111 Alamy Stock Photo:** Don Johnston_MA. **111 Dorling Kindersley:** Abby Cook (x3). **Getty Images / iStock:** Dmitr1ch (c). **112 Dorling Kindersley:** Abby Cook. **Dreamstime.com:** Outdoorsman (tc); Planetfelicity (cra). **Getty Images / iStock:** Dmitr1ch (cb). **113 Dreamstime.com:** Andreanita (tc); Cherylramalho (bl). **Getty Images:** Natphotos / Photodisc (cb). **NASA:** Michael Studinger (cl). **Shutterstock.com:** PhotoscapeArt (cra). **114 Alamy Stock Photo:** Don Johnston_MA (tl). **Dorling Kindersley:** Abby Cook (cr). **114–115 Alamy Stock Photo:** Jason Pineau / All Canada Photos (b). **Dreamstime.com:** Tihomir Trifonov. **115 Dreamstime.com:** Dasya11 (clb). **Shutterstock.com:** Nick Pecker (t); Richard Seeley (ca); Wirestock Creators (cr). **116–117 Dreamstime.com:** Suse Schulz (t). **116 Dreamstime.com:** Stephan Pietzko (bc). **Getty Images / iStock:** Dmitr1ch (t). **117 Getty Images / iStock:** victormaschek (bl). **Shutterstock.com:** muratart (cr); Tracey Mendenhall Porreca (br). **118 Alamy Stock Photo:** Tawna Brown (clb). **Dorling Kindersley:** Abby Cook (c). **Dreamstime.com:** (cra); Olga Popova (br). **Getty Images:** Darren Keast / 500px (cl). **118–119 Dreamstime.com:** Tihomir Trifonov. **119 Alamy Stock Photo:** Dominique Braud / Dembinsky Photo Associates / Alamy (b). **Dorling Kindersley:** Abby Cook (tl); David Tipling (cla). **Dreamstime.com:** Hayley Linton (tr). **120 Alamy Stock Photo:** Michael Nolan / Robertharding (cl). **Shutterstock.com:** FloridaStock (bc). **120–121 Kyra St. Pierre:** (t). **121 Alamy Stock Photo:** Eric Baccega / agefotostock (bl); Wolfgang Kaehler (br). **122 Alamy Stock Photo:** (cr). **Dorling Kindersley:** Abby Cook (tr). **Getty Images:** Cavan Images (clb); Jan-Stefan Knick / EyeEm (br). **122–123 Dreamstime.com:** Tihomir Trifonov. **123 Alamy Stock Photo:** Louise Murray (tl). **Dorling Kindersley:** Abby Cook (b). **Dreamstime.com:** Debra Millet (cra). **Getty Images / iStock:** Pchoui / E+ (c). **124 Dorling Kindersley:** Abby Cook (tr). **125 Dorling Kindersley:** Abby Cook (b). **126 Dorling Kindersley:** Abby Cook (t). **127 Dorling Kindersley:** Abby Cook (bc); Abby Cook (br); Abby Cook (br/tree); Abby Cook (fbr). **128 Dorling Kindersley:** Abby Cook (tl); Abby Cook (br).

Cover images: *Front*: **Alamy Stock Photo:** Ronald Wittek / agefotostock c; **Dorling Kindersley:** Abby Cook crb, Abby Cook cla/ (Art); **Dreamstime.com:** Rejean Bedard clb, Barbara Burns bl, Anatoly Kazakov tl, Leerobin clb/ (Flower), Sergio Llaguno br, William Mahnken cr, Openrangestock tc, Sean Pavone t, Sdbower cl, Snehitdesign cra, Taigis ca, Wirestock cla/ (Bear); **Shutterstock.com:** Brian A Wolf cla; *Back*: **Alamy Stock Photo:** Westend61 GmbH clb; **Dreamstime.com:** Lukas Bischoff t, Steve Cole crb, Ben Graham bl, Mariusz Jurgielewicz cb, Petar Kremenarov tc, Lunamarina cr, Oliclimb br, Jason Ondreicka cla, Stockoxinoxi ca, Natali Suietska cra, Craig Taylor cl; *Spine*: **Dorling Kindersley:** Abby Cook t, Abby Cook ca; **Dreamstime.com:** Ivan Kokoulin b.

All other images © Dorling Kindersley
For further information see: www.dkimages.com